YOU CAN'T BEAT THE HOURS

Books by Mel Allen

YOU CAN'T BEAT THE HOURS (with Ed Fitzgerald)
IT TAKES HEART (with Frank Graham, Jr.)

You Can't Beat

A Long, Loving Look at Big-League Baseball—

MEL ALLEN *and*

Harper & Row, Publishers

the Hours

Including Some Yankees I Have Known

ED FITZGERALD

New York, Evanston, and London

The verse on page 19 is reprinted by permission of John Kieran. It originally appeared in the *New York Times*.

The poem on page 37 by Edgar A. Guest is reprinted by permission of the Reilly & Lee Company.

Why do I like baseball?
The pay is good,
it keeps you out in the fresh air and sunshine, and
you can't beat the hours.

—TIM HURST

A section of illustrations follows page 84. These photographs are used through the courtesy of *Sport* magazine; also, the New York Yankees, United Press, Nat Fein–*Herald Tribune*, United States Navy.

YOU CAN'T BEAT THE HOURS

Chapter 1

Sometimes I think Mel was born with a
baseball in his mouth.—ANNA LEIBOVITZ ISRAEL

MY first season as a broadcaster of New York Yankee
baseball games was a long time ago, 1939 to be exact, and on Opening Day at the Stadium the Yankees beat the Boston Red Sox, 2–0.
Bill Dickey hit a home run for the Yankees and Red Ruffing
pitched for them. The losing pitcher was Lefty Grove. The Boston
shortstop and player-manager was Joe Cronin, who is now the president of the American League, and the Boston right fielder was a
rookie playing his first big-league game, a tall, skinny kid named
Ted Williams who looked pretty good hitting a double off the right-
field fence.

It was a long time ago, all right. The Yankees' batting order had
Frank Crosetti leading off and playing short; Red Rolfe at third;
Jake Powell in left field; Joe DiMaggio in center; Lou Gehrig,
starting what turned out to be his last season and playing in his
2,124th consecutive game, at first base; Bill Dickey catching; a
rookie just out of Manhattan College, Joe Gallagher, in right; Joe
Gordon at second base; and Charlie Ruffing doing the pitching. The
parade out to the flagpole before the game was led by the Mayor of

1

the City of New York, Fiorello H. LaGuardia, and LaGuardia threw out the first ball.

The world that was reflected on the front page of the *New York Times* that morning seems even longer ago because so much has happened since then. The World's Fair at Flushing Meadows was getting ready for its official opening, and on Opening Day they dedicated the RCA pavilion there. The *pièce de résistance* of the dedication ceremonies was a demonstration of the new communications miracle, television, which, the RCA executives said, would someday be in every American home. Adolf Hitler had called the German Reichstag into special session to deal with the worsening international situation, and Senator David I. Walsh of Massachusetts had warned the United States that we could no longer defend a two-ocean country with a one-ocean Navy and that we had better remain strictly neutral in the European crisis. The hit show on Broadway was *Leave It to Me,* starring Sophie Tucker, William Gaxton and Victor Moore, and some of the critics were excited about a blonde in the show, Mary Martin, who sang a number called "My Heart Belongs to Daddy." The big movies starred Don Ameche in *The Story of Alexander Graham Bell* and Mickey Rooney in *Huckleberry Finn.* The book everybody was talking about was *The Grapes of Wrath* by John Steinbeck, and the hottest program on the radio was *Information, Please.* The A&P was selling eggs for twenty-two cents a dozen, you could buy a new Buick for $894 f.o.b. Flint, Michigan, and Hearn's Department Store advertised a case of gin for $12.32. You know it was a long time ago.

It was a pretty good ball game, with fine pitching by Ruffing and Grove and two spectacular catches in center field by DiMaggio. The weather had been gray and threatening in the morning but the sky cleared at noon and it turned out to be a pleasant afternoon. The 7th Regiment band played for the pregame ceremonies and the crowd got a big kick out of Mayor LaGuardia marching all the way out to the flagpole and back with the ballplayers, who were even sloppier

in their marching than the boys are today—which is understandable
when you consider that almost every man in the league today has
had some sort of military training. Then there was another treat for
the crowd when Babe Ruth showed up at about three o'clock. Like
the rest of us in the stands and the press box, Babe must have had a
twinge watching Lou Gehrig go through a bad day. Gehrig didn't
get a hit, bounced into two double plays, and gave Ruffing a head-
ache in the ninth by letting a peg from the infield get knocked out
of his mitt for the Yankees' only error of the game. Ruffing hung
on, though, and kept his shutout, and the Yankees proved that they
were going to be able to survive nicely and keep right on winning
even with me up in the radio booth calling the play-by-play.

They haven't done badly, for a fact. In the first 25 years of my
broadcasting for them, they managed to win 18 pennants and 13
world championships. How about that?

I did the games that first year as assistant to Arch McDonald, who
moved to Washington the next season to broadcast for the Senators.
It wasn't my first professional assignment. I had been in New York,
working as a network announcer for the Columbia Broadcasting
System, since January, 1936. But I was a long way from home, home
being Alabama, where I was born in Birmingham on St. Valentine's
Day of 1913. My father, Julius Allen Israel, and my mother, Anna
Leibovitz, had been married in Milwaukee and then moved south.
By the time I was born, a year later, Dad, having learned the business from his father, was pretty well established in a dry-goods
business of his own in Johns, Alabama, a little mining-district
town about 25 miles southwest of the big steel city, Bessemer. Dad
moved his business every time he saw a chance to improve things,
so we went from Johns to Sylacauga to Bessemer, and then, a few
years after World War I, to Cordova, Alabama.

We didn't have too easy a time of it in Cordova. Dad had sold his
business in Bessemer for about $20,000, and he lost all of it in Cor-
dova. When it was all gone, he had to go to work as a salesman, sell-

ing shirts on the road. Later he moved us all to Greensboro, North Carolina, and that's where, after being crazy about baseball as long as I can remember, I finally got close to the game. There was a minor-league club in town, the Greensboro Patriots, and when I was eleven years old I got a job as their batboy. Jim Turner was one of their pitchers and the next time I saw him was in 1940, when he joined the Yankees in Florida for spring training. Typical of pitchers, he had a long memory and told me all about my earlier hitch as a batboy.

My mother took a dim view of my interest in baseball, mostly because she wanted me to be a musician—a concert violinist, as a matter of fact. I thought she would forget about that when I almost cut off the forefinger on my left hand paring a peach one day, but all she did was decide that if I couldn't be a violinist I could at least be a cornetist. I was reasonably faithful about my music lessons but I was a lot more faithful to baseball. I remained so when we moved again, this time back to Alabama—to Birmingham—where I finished high school and got ready to enter the University of Alabama. I was on the high school baseball, basketball and football teams, but I liked baseball best.

When I started at the university I was only fifteen years old. I stayed there eight years, earning my B.A. in 1932 and my law degree in 1936. Dad moved the whole family to Tuscaloosa, the university town, because there wasn't enough money to put me up in a dormitory. To help out a little, I worked every Saturday as a shoe salesman in Brown's Dollar Store. It was a lucky thing for me that I had to take every opportunity to earn a dollar, because that's how I got started as an announcer. Actually, the way it began was that I didn't make the varsity baseball squad, so I turned my hand to intramural baseball, the drama club, and writing sports for the school paper. By the time I was a senior I was sports editor of both the newspaper and the annual magazine. Later, when I was a law student, I worked as a correspondent for out-of-town Alabama newspapers and did the public-address system announcing for Alabama's home football games.

One Saturday morning in 1935, Frank Thomas, the football coach, was asked by a Birmingham radio station to nominate somebody to serve through the season as broadcaster for both the Alabama and Auburn football games. The man who had been doing the job had left. Coach Thomas suggested me, and the $5-per-game fee looked good to me, so even though I wasn't sure I could do it, I accepted. The station manager hired me after one audition in which I tried to re-create the play-by-play of the 1927 Rose Bowl game between Alabama and Stanford, which Alabama tied, 7–7, in the last minute of play. It worked out pretty well, I think, although I remember that in one of the first games I did I got the downs mixed up pretty badly. What happened was that I completely lost track of one down. I was calling it third down coming up when the scoreboard said fourth down. To get even, I hastily ran off an imaginary line buck while Alabama was still in the huddle. Then, when they came out of the huddle and got up over the ball, I was all ready to call the fourth-down play.

It was some time before it ever occurred to me that I might be able to make a living talking into a microphone. I was on a vacation trip to New York during the week before Christmas, 1936, a reasonably footloose young man with a law degree in his pocket but not much else, when I stopped in to take a tour of the Columbia Broadcasting System studios. I told one of the men I met there that I had done some play-by-play broadcasting for the CBS station in Birmingham, and he seemed interested. He even invited me to audition, so they could see what I sounded like. I thought it would be an interesting experience, so I did it. I didn't expect anything to come of it, and I was completely taken by surprise when they ended up offering me a job. I told them I already had a job, which I did, teaching speech classes at the university for $1,800 a year, but when they said CBS would pay me $45 a week, or about $10 a week more

than I was making, I was tempted. I said I would think about it
when I got back home and would let them know.

It didn't surprise me any that my father, when he heard about it,
came as close to exploding as it is possible for him to come. "It's just
plain foolishness for you to go all the way through college and law
school for eight years, and work as hard as you've worked, just to
throw it all away talking on the radio," he said. He didn't think
much, either, of the fact that the CBS men had suggested that I
ought to change my name. "What's so bad about Mel Israel?" he
wanted to know. I told him there wasn't anything bad about it,
but that the radio people didn't think it was euphonious enough, or
easy enough on the ears, for a professional radio announcer. "I'll
borrow your middle name," I told him one day when we were in the
middle of the same old argument. "I'll call myself Mel Allen." He
didn't mind that so much, and he was beginning to give in all along
the line, although he plainly didn't believe me when I kept insisting
that I just wanted to try it for a year or so, that it would be wonderful experience for me in whatever I did later on. "You'll never come
back," he said prophetically. "If you go to New York, you'll never
come back."

He was right. I never went back to Alabama, except to work or
to visit, but thank goodness he and Mom and my brother Larry and
my sister Esther all were willing, after a while, to move to New
York.

Like the newest recruit in any business, who always gets the
meanest job with the worst hours, I started out at CBS opening up
the network's morning programming by introducing organ selections on what we referred to as the Mighty Wurlitzer. A couple of
months later I caught on as the regular announcer for a sponsored
nighttime show, and my salary went all the way up to $95 a week.
I was beginning to have my doubts about going back to Alabama.
Also, I liked New York. How could anybody not like New York?
Everything about it, the buildings, the crowds of people in the

streets, the theaters, the restaurants, the taxicabs, the ball games, the lavish stores, the magnificent hotels, dazzled me. It made me feel that I was somebody just to be a part of it. Tuscaloosa was never like this.

Things were even more exciting after I got my first real break. In those days a network, shut out of a major event when one of the others had bought up the exclusive broadcasting rights, thought nothing of pirating a report even though they weren't allowed to set up their equipment at the scene. So, when NBC got an exclusive on the big Vanderbilt Cup automobile race on Long Island, CBS sent me up in a twin-engined airplane to cover the race as best I could by looking down on it. You might say I was doing an over-the-spot, if not an on-the-spot, report. It might not have been so difficult if it hadn't rained, but it did rain, and eventually the race was called off. Not right away, though. Before the word came through that it was off, I had filled up almost an hour of air time talking about nothing. Anybody who has listened to me over the years probably is going to doubt this, but it wasn't easy to do all that talking without having any idea what I was going to say next. But I managed to get through it, and the people I worked for not only were pleased that I had saved the network from worse embarrassment but also were convinced that I was a natural for sports broadcasting. I had proved, they thought, that I had the first requisite of every play-by-play sports announcer: the resourcefulness to keep going and to hold the interest of the audience without the help of a script. Many times since, on rainy afternoons at Yankee Stadium with the people in the field boxes huddling under umbrellas while pools of water collected in the huge tarpaulins covering the infield, I have had to improvise for even longer stretches of time than I did the day I was flying over the Vanderbilt Cup course. But it has never been quite so frightening as it was that first time.

The nicest part of talking about the Yankees is that there isn't anything else I would rather be doing. That's a miraculous thing

for any man to be able to say about what he does for a living, but
just as it's true for Tom Tresh out there on the field, hitting the
ball and catching it and throwing it to help the Yankees win the
ball game, it's true for me up in the broadcasting booth, doing
everything I can to help the Yankee fans enjoy the game as much
as possible. If I had realized my first ambition, which was to be a
big-league ballplayer, I would have played one position. As it is,
I play all nine—and even occasionally umpire! I love it. It has
always been that way, ever since the season of 1939 when I
was given the number two place behind Arch McDonald broadcasting both the New York Yankee and New York Giant home
games. Arch moved over to the Washington Senators the next
year, as I said, and I worked the Yankee games with J. C.
Flippen and the Giant games with Joe Bolton. Connie Desmond,
who later had a long run broadcasting for the Dodgers with Red
Barber and Vince Scully, was my partner in 1941. It was possible
to handle both the Yankee and Giant home games because the two
clubs were never at home at the same time, the same situation which
exists today with the Yankees and the Mets in New York, the
White Sox and the Cubs in Chicago, and the Dodgers and the
Angels in Los Angeles.

Along with just about everybody else, I found myself in the
army in 1941, a private in the infantry. I made staff sergeant after
a couple of years and then was transferred into the Armed Forces
Radio Service as an announcer on the *Army Hour* radio program.
After I was discharged early in 1946, I couldn't wait to get back to
baseball. I was supposed to rejoin the Giants but they had trouble
getting a station outlet. Larry MacPhail, running the Yankees,
asked me if I wanted to handle their games, and I said sure. Who
wouldn't? The two clubs had agreed to do their broadcasts separately, so that each could do its road games live, and I persuaded
Russ Hodges to join me on the Yankee job. I'm sure Russ, who
since has become Mr. Giant, never was sorry. I know I never have
been.

Sometimes my mother says she isn't so sure it has been all for the best, but all she really means is that she wishes I would get married. She's afraid that I spend so much time on my job that I'll never get around to meeting a nice girl and marrying her. It isn't only Mom; everybody in the family seems to spend most of their waking hours trying to marry me off. The newspapermen don't help any, either, by always referring to me as one of the most eligible bachelors around. Actually, when you consider that I was born way back there in 1913, I think I must be getting to the point where most girls would consider me too old to be eligible for anything except a rocking chair.

Tom Meany, one of the best sportswriters in the business, and now, after a hitch with Bob Fishel's Yankee publicity staff, doing publicity work with the Mets, has probably had the last word on my reputation as a nonmarrier. I showed up at one of the Yankees' victory parties one night with a good-looking girl on my arm, and Meany said, "Here comes Mel Allen with the future Miss Jones."

Mom's best crack on the subject was made when a magazine writer asked her if she was happy about the way my life had gone. "I wish he was a shoemaker," she told him. "A married shoemaker."

I guess the only other thing Mom doesn't particularly like about the way I make a living is the inevitable criticism that goes along with the job. Like the ballplayer's wife, who squirms when she hears somebody in the stands call her man a big bum, it hurts Mom to hear somebody complain that I'm a Yankee-lover, that I talk too much, that my puns are terrible and that my grammar is a disgrace. I can understand her feeling that way but it doesn't bother me. I always remember what former President Harry Truman said on the subject of criticism. "If you can't stand the heat, get out of the kitchen." That's the way you have to look at it when you're doing a job that keeps you in the public eye all the time.

You have to be able, too, to enjoy the multitude of events you are asked to attend. In one off-season month my invitation book has included: an interfaith luncheon in Bethlehem, Pennsylvania;

an assembly at the Berriman Junior High School in Brooklyn with the theme "to inspire youth to reach for goals seemingly beyond their grasp"; the annual football banquet of the University of Notre Dame; the Norwalk Jewish Center sports dinner; the annual dinner of the Greenwich Old Timers Athletic Association; the annual Father-Son Dinner of the Holy Name Society of the Holy Family Church in Flushing, New York; the annual football banquet of the University of Alabama; the Kiwanis Sports Night in Winsted, Connecticut; the annual awards dinner of the B'nai B'rith Lodge of New York; the campaign meeting of the Salvation Army of New York; the sports dinner of the St. John the Evangelist Church of New Haven, Connecticut; the Touchdown Club dinner in Columbus, Ohio; the annual dinner of the University of Miami Gridiron Club in Coral Gables, Florida; and the annual dance of the Chief Justice White Council, Knights of Columbus, of Teaneck, New Jersey.

So far as criticism is concerned, it's silly to get mad at the kind that consists mostly of quoting your own words, so what I do instead is try to learn from such pieces. I don't lose any sleep over them, though. I figure that anybody who talks into a microphone as much as I do is bound to say some silly things every now and then. Like the time somebody caught me saying, "We have now reached that stage of the game where every pitch must be considered by the pitcher with the utmost care. In other words, there is no room for margin of error." Or the time I had the wrong catcher in the game for eight innings and then had to account for him coming in as a pinch-hitter in the ninth.

Sometimes criticism can make you feel downright good. For instance, after the 1952 Notre Dame–Oklahoma football game, I got almost a thousand letters and telegrams from Oklahoma fans accusing me of being biased in favor of Notre Dame and almost a thousand letters and telegrams from Notre Dame fans accusing me of being biased in favor of Oklahoma. I'll take that kind of criticism any time.

The big rap hung on me, of course, is that I root for the Yankees in my broadcasts. My honest answer to this one, which I sometimes think I have to give a couple of hundred times a week, is that I am partisan but not prejudiced. Partisanship, I think, is all right. It gives color and excitement to a broadcast, and it makes the home-town fans happy. Prejudice would be unpardonable and I hope never to be guilty of it. I don't think a prejudiced broadcaster could survive in New York, anyway. The city is too cosmopolitan for that kind of approach. It's hard enough to get by just being a Yankee partisan. After all, the city used to have the Giants and the Dodgers, with all of their millions of fans, and has the Mets, now, plus nobody knows how many Indian, Tiger, Cardinal, Brave, Red Sox and every other kind of fans. They keep me in line.

In the first inning of the second game of the 1958 World Series, I was working hard telling everybody about the way the Milwaukee Braves were clobbering the Yankees. (They got seven runs off them in that inning.) And while we were talking through a wait for the second Yankee relief pitcher of the inning to come in, one of the fellows in the booth shoved a telegram in front of me. It was from a man in Boston, and it said, "Quit yapping, you Yankee-lover. You're talking too much. Just let me watch the game." At first it bothered me, but then I noticed that the telegram had been sent two hours before the game had even started. So I just threw it away.

I don't believe he ever said it, but if he did, I would also have to classify the Yogi Berra story as one of my favorite pieces of Mel Allen criticism. Bill Davidson, writing in *Look* magazine, claimed: "When I asked Yogi Berra what he thought of Allen as a sports-caster, the Yankee veteran's reply was a masterpiece of primitive simplicity. Said Yogi, 'Too many woids.'" Like a lot of other Berra stories, I suspect somebody simply made that one up because it sounded like something Yogi should have said.

I plead guilty to the charge that I am a ferocious punner. I just can't help it. I admit that sometimes when I'm confronted later with what I said over the air I'm embarrassed, but at the time it always seems like a good idea. Like, for instance, the St. Patrick's Day Sunday a year or so ago when we were playing an exhibition game against the Reds at Al Lopez Field in Tampa. (Al lives in the Ybor City section of Tampa and is a big local hero.) We were sending the game back to New York by television as well as radio, and there was a lot of trouble with the picture because of a power failure. That's always a problem for an announcer. You hate to keep repeating yourself but you have to explain frequently what's wrong with the picture or else the viewer will think it's his set that's on the blink and start calling the repairman. So, after spending half the afternoon talking about the trouble with the power lines, I couldn't resist saying, when Mickey Mantle came up and hit a long home run for the Yankees, "Well, that was one time we didn't have any power failure."

Anyway, what I wanted to say was that, puns, criticism, mistakes and all, I've enjoyed every year I've spent with the Yankees, and at the end of the 1963 season there had been exactly twenty-five of them. I still approach every ball game with a full charge of eagerness and anticipation. I still get a kick out of kids asking me for my autograph just as though I were a ballplayer. I still get all worked up over a great catch, a booming home run that really goes out of there, a fine job of pitching, or a double play made the hard way. I still can't quite believe that every day in the week I can walk into the ball park for nothing and get paid for watching the New York Yankees play baseball.

Chapter 2

There's something about the Yankee uniform
that gets you. I think it's the wool—
it itches.—JOHN GALLAGHER

ONE of the few things I regret about my long association with the Yankees is that it didn't begin just a little sooner than it did. It must have been New Year's Eve and Mardi Gras combined every day around the ball club when Babe Ruth was in the lineup, not to mention Lou Gehrig, Bob Meusel, Earle Combs, Tony Lazzeri, Jumping Joe Dugan and the rest. The Yankees have had a lot of great ball clubs, and I've had the good luck to be around several of them, but I don't think any team had more to do with the building of the Yankee tradition than the 1927 club. This was the gang of sluggers for which the expressive term "Murderers' Row" was coined, and a more truculent batting order would be hard to imagine. Earle Combs was the lead-off man, and Mark Koenig the number two hitter. Then the poor pitcher got George Herman Ruth, who not only hit 60 home runs that year but also managed to put together a batting average of .356. After that it was Lou Gehrig, the cleanup man, a .373 hitter in 1927, with 47 home runs, 18 triples and 52 doubles in his bag of 218 hits. And then Bob Meusel, Tony Lazzeri, Joe Dugan and Benny Bengough. The pitcher might be Herb Pennock or George Pipgras or Waite Hoyte or Urban Shocker or Wilcy Moore. It was some ball club.

Paul Gallico once wrote: "I used to sit in the press box with my heart in my throat, my palms sweaty, my mouth all dry and cottony, and my nerves prickly and on edge, watching the Yankees play. It was like when I was a kid and there used to be a lot of blasting going on down on Park Avenue where they were digging out the cut for the New York Central tracks. There would be a laborer with a box with a plunger handle, and they would spread the mats and get ready to dynamite. There would be a nerve-racking suspense and what seemed like an interminable wait. But you knew that eventually he would push that handle down and then there would be one hell of a big *boom* and chunks of Park Avenue would go flying through the air. Well, it was just like that with the 1927 Yankees. You never knew when that batting order was going to push the handle down. But when it went, you could hear the explosion all the way to South Albany, and when the smoke cleared away, the poor old opposing pitcher wouldn't be there any more. And Yankees would be legging it over the plate with runs, sometimes in single file but more often in bunches of twos and threes as home runs cleared the bases and they could get together and chat comfortably on the way in."

"The Reign of Terror" is what the newspapermen called the time when that ball club was tearing the league apart. It was an accurate description. My favorite story about these fencebusters isn't about any of the great games they played but about a batting practice. It was at Forbes Field in Pittsburgh the day before the first game of the '27 World Series. The Pirates went through a long workout and then generously extended the courtesy of the field to the Yankees. The Pirates took their showers and got dressed and then came back out to watch the Yankees go through their paces. They would have been better off going straight home because what they saw must have kept them awake all night. One after another, Miller Huggins' big fellows stepped up to the plate and hammered the ball out of sight. It was home run or nothing, and nothing that the Pirate ball-players had ever heard about the Yankees compared with the sight of the real thing. These were big, powerful men, and as they wheeled and pivoted in the batting cage, lashing out at the ball, with wrists as thick as the branches of a tree, the people who lived on the streets back of the ball park must have thought it was raining base-balls. Little 140-pound Lloyd Waner, the fine Pittsburgh outfielder, turned to his brother Paul, one of the great hitters in baseball history, and said, "Gee, they're awful big guys. Do they always hit like that?"

Whether the Yankees had deliberately staged their demonstration to put a little fear into the Pirates' hearts, or whether it was just one of those things, the New York reporter who described the unusual scene in his dispatch that night, and ended by saying that the Pirates were thoroughly shell-shocked and the Series was as good as over right now, knew what he was talking about. The Yankees won it in four straight. Barney Dreyfuss, the owner of the Pirates, said, "No championship club of one major league is so good that it should take four straight from the pennant winner of the other league." But Barney was wrong. The Yankees of 1927 were that good. (And what about the Los Angeles Dodgers of 1963, who humiliated the Yankees in exactly the same fashion, much to the astonishment of the whole baseball world and the rich satisfaction of part of it?) They were still that good in 1928, when they lambasted the St. Louis Cardinals in four straight for their second clean sweep in a row. That was the Series in which Babe Ruth hit .625, with three home runs and three doubles in his ten hits. Lou Gehrig didn't do quite so well. He hit only .545. He did hit four homers, though, so he didn't have to turn in his uniform.

Another thing that would have happened to me if I had gone to work for the Yankees sooner than I did is that I would have had the pleasure of working for the gentleman who built the ball club, Colonel Jacob Ruppert. I just missed working for him. Colonel Ruppert died at his home on Fifth Avenue in New York on January 13, 1939, the year I began broadcasting at the Stadium. His association with the Yankees had lasted for twenty-four years.

Colonel Ruppert and Captain (later Colonel) Tillinghast Huston, who became friends because they were both enthusiastic New York Giant fans and their season boxes were located close together at the Polo Grounds, bought the Yankee franchise in January, 1915. They paid a little less than half a million dollars for it. The two men were almost exact opposites. Ruppert was a shrewd, autocratic businessman who set great store by careful organization and sound discipline, and Huston was a carefree adventurer who was interested first, last and always in having a good time. They were both used to having their own way, and before very long they were fighting all the time. They differed on almost every question that came up, and it was inevitable that the day would come when they would agree to disagree permanently. The fact that they fought bitterly over Ruppert's hiring of Miller Huggins to manage the Yankees in 1918, when Huston wanted Wilbert Robinson of the Dodgers to get the job, didn't really matter very much. If it hadn't been that, it would have been something else. It was an important milestone in the history of the club when Ruppert paid Huston $1,500,000 for his stock on May 21, 1923, and became the sole owner of the Yankees.

It was from Ruppert that the Yankee tradition of perfectionism, of pride in organization and pride in self, of playing only to win and the hell with second place, stems. The Colonel always said that his idea of a good ball game was one in which the Yankees had a 13-run lead in the top of the ninth with two out and two strikes on the hitter. He would do anything within his power to improve the team, to help it win more pennants by bigger margins. If the Colonel were alive today, he would nod gravely and show no surprise at all to learn that when the Yankees won the 1963 pennant it marked the twenty-eighth time they had earned the right to fly that emblem

from the Yankee Stadium flagpole. Ruppert expected the Yankees
to win. That, in his view, was the only reason for playing. He could
be gracious in defeat, because he was a gentleman, but he didn't like
it. His ballplayers learned not to like it either.

They tell a lot of stories about the old Colonel but I think my
favorite is the one Waite Hoyt, a great pitcher for the Yankees in
the 1920's and now a fine broadcaster for the Cincinnati Reds, tells.
Hoyt used to earn a good salary for winning twenty games or so a
year for the Yankees, but he always thought he ought to get more
money. Once, when he couldn't get together with Ruppert's general
manager, Ed Barrow, on a new contract, he talked Barrow into letting him take a trip uptown to Ruppert's Brewery in the Bronx to
talk it over with the owner himself. The brewery was operating
even in those Prohibition days, making what was euphemistically
known as near beer, a product that the humorist Bugs Baer once
said must have been named by a very poor judge of distance. The
Colonel was busy and Hoyt had to wait in the reception room for
half an hour, where he occupied himself by looking at pictures of
Ruppert's baronial estate in Garrison, New York, the brewery, and
half a dozen New York City office buildings the Colonel owned. It
was an impressive display, and it left Waite totally unprepared for
Ruppert's answer to his request for a more favorable contract.

"Be reasonable, Hoyt," the Colonel said in his thick German ac-
cent. "Everybody comes asking me for more money. Ruth wants
more money. Gehrig wants more money. You want more money.
What do you fellows think I am, a millionaire?"

Hoyt figures in another story that illustrates Colonel Ruppert's
insatiable passion for winning. "What's the matter with you,
Hoyt?" he complained one day when he met Waite in the Stadium
offices. "You win all the time but you win one to nothing, two to
one, three to two. It's always close. Why can't you do like Pennock
and Shawkey? They win their games nine to one and twelve to
nothing. If I was you I would try to do better already."

The Colonel wasn't kidding. He took baseball and the Yankees very seriously indeed, a trait which led him to see nothing comical in the sight of Casey Stengel, then a weather-beaten outfielder for the Giants, thumbing his nose playfully at the Yankee bench as he ran around the bases on one of the home runs he hit to win a couple of games in the 1923 World Series. Ruppert was so angry at this display of amiable contempt that he filed a complaint with Judge Landis. Stengel, he said, should be punished for unseemly conduct on the ball field. But the old Judge, who was always pretty good at guessing public opinion, didn't see it that way. "When a ballplayer breaks up a World Series game with a home run like that," he said wisely, "he should be permitted a certain amount of exuberance and self-expression."

It's too bad the Colonel had no way of knowing then that Casey Stengel would end up hanging ten American League championship pennants from the roof of Yankee Stadium. He would have forgiven him anything.

Of course, the most exciting part of being with the Yankees in the 1920's and the early 1930's would have been seeing Babe Ruth and Lou Gehrig hit that ball, watching them demoralize every card-carrying member of the pitchers' union and make the Yankees the kings of baseball.

There was only one Babe Ruth. Roger Maris, another fine Yankee, hit 61 home runs in 1961, and that's one more than Ruth hit in 1927, even if Maris did have a 162-game season going for him against Ruth's 154 games. Somebody else may very well break Maris' record one of these days, but Babe Ruth still is and always will be the home-run champion. It isn't only that he hit 714 home runs in his incredible career, it's the inimitable flair and the bombastic authority with which he did it. "The Ruth is mighty and shall prevail," Heywood Broun wrote many years ago, and that was the simple truth. He dominated the game with his outsized personality as much as with his home-run bat. He was a national hero in the grand manner. It made sense that, years after Ruth had retired from the game, a Japanese infantryman, eager to shout an insult at the Americans facing him across a malarial field on Guadalcanal in the early days of World War II, screamed furiously, "To hell with Babe Ruth!" It even made sense that Ruth, criticized for holding out for an $80,000 contract in 1930, and asked why he thought he should be paid more money than the $75,000 salary of the President of the United States, should grin and say, "Why not? I had a better year than he had."

It doesn't make any difference whether or not he actually called his shot on the celebrated home run he hit off Charley Root of the Chicago Cubs in the 1932 World Series; it was the kind of thing you expected Babe Ruth to do, and it is impossible to work up any interest in the old argument. Calling his shot like that, and then making good on it, was a Ruthian act. You wouldn't believe it of anybody else, but there wasn't anybody else like the Babe. John Kieran once said it in a poem:

He was Bogey Man for the pitching clan, and he clubbed them soon and late;
He manned his guns and hit home runs from here to the Golden Gate.
With vim and verve he walloped the curve from Texas to Duluth;
Which is no small task, and I rise to ask: Was there ever a guy like Ruth?

Fred Haney, the general manager of the Los Angeles Angels, remembers hitting a home run at Yankee Stadium when he was a rookie infielder with the St. Louis Browns. It wasn't much of a home run, a low slice that just managed to stay inside the right-field foul line and plop into the seats. But it was a home run, and when the inning ended and Babe Ruth ran past him on his way into the Yankee dugout, Fred bragged about it a little. "Hey, Babe," he hollered, "how did you like that? Now you're only forty-nine ahead of me!" The Babe didn't say anything, but the next time he got up he hit one a country mile, a soaring, majestic, authentic Ruth home run to deep center field. Rounding third, where Haney was standing dejectedly, the Babe laughed out loud. "How do we stand now, kid?" he said.

It has always interested me that Babe Ruth, the free-swinging slugging man, finished up with a lifetime batting average of .342, a mark exceeded on the roster of the immortals by only six men—Ty Cobb, Rogers Hornsby, big Dan Brouthers, Ed Delahanty, Willie Keeler and Tris Speaker. You don't think of Ruth in connection with batting-average exploits, and in fact he won the batting championship of the American League only once, with .378 in 1924, but his lifetime average is higher than that of Bill Terry, George Sisler, Paul Waner, Honus Wagner and Frank Frisch. "Shucks," the Babe said once, "I coulda hit a .400 lifetime average easy. But I would've had to hit them singles. I was gettin' paid to hit home runs."

Sure he was. And he did it with a special flourish. Like the time the Yankees were playing the White Sox in Chicago, and the game went into extra innings and dragged on and on, tied 1–1, into the top of the fifteenth. Ruth was due up third in the inning, and as he ran in from the field, Mark Roth, the Yankees' traveling secretary, yelled at him, "Hey, you guys better get us out of here this inning or we're gonna miss our train home!" The Babe called back cheerfully, "Okay, Mark, I'll take care of it." And, naturally, the truth about Babe Ruth being even stranger than Frank Merriwell fiction, the Babe stepped up there against Mike Cvengros and smashed the ball into the right-field stands. Climbing into the bus that was to rush them to the railroad station, the Babe said, seriously, to Roth, "You should've told me about that earlier, Mark."

Then there was the home run he hit for Johnny Sylvester, the classic—and the original—of all the stories ever told about big-league ballplayers promising to hit home runs for sick or crippled boys. It's the kind of story that you have to tell with unashamed sentiment; you don't dare touch it up with a dash of cynicism. You have to picture the Babe as he really was, a huge, unshapely man weighing about 220 pounds, a bearlike body supported by legs so slim as to be almost spindly, an unusually large head, like a big, round ball on his massive shoulders, a squat-featured face with an oversized, pushed-in nose, and a heart even bigger than his body.

The Babe was always willing to do something for somebody, or anything for anybody. So it is completely understandable that when he was asked—nobody has ever been sure who asked him—to make a trip to New Jersey to pay a visit to a seriously ill boy who idolized him, he said, sure, he'd go. Thirteen-year-old Johnny Sylvester had had a grave operation and wasn't recovering as well as his doctor thought he should. The doctor and his father both thought that maybe a visit from his hero, the Babe, would be just the medicine Johnny needed. So the morning after the telephone call to the Babe, the door to young Johnny's hospital room opened and Babe Ruth walked in. Babe Ruth? Writing about it after the story became known, Paul Gallico said, "It was God himself who walked into the room, straight from His glittering throne, God dressed in a camel's hair polo coat and camel's hair cap, God with a flat nose and little piggy eyes and a big grin, and a fat, black cigar sticking out of the side of it."

Babe talked to Johnny for as long as the doctor would let him, and he signed a baseball for him, and then, just before he left, he did the only other thing it came into his head to do for the boy. He promised him that he would hit a home run for him in the ball game that afternoon. That's a dangerous thing to promise, unless you don't expect the boy to take you literally or to be crushed with disappointment if you don't come through. But Babe knew that Johnny Sylvester was a very sick boy, and he knew that Johnny was taking him quite seriously indeed and that he would be holding him to his promise every time he came to bat that afternoon. A lesser man might wish he had never said it, might push it to the back of his mind, might even rationalize that the next time he happened to hit a home run, whenever it might be, he could call up Johnny Sylvester and tell him that that one was for him. But Babe Ruth went to the ball park knowing he was under contract to hit a home run. It was very much on his mind when he went to bat against Flint Rhem of the Browns in the last half of the first inning.

He lashed out at the first pitch with every controlled ounce of his incredible strength, and he drove the ball 430 feet into the right-center-field seats. With that burden lifted from his back, the Babe hit another home run off Rhem, and then, in the sixth, he caught hold of a 3-and-2 pitch by Herman Bell for his third home run of the day. Johnny Sylvester slept well in his hospital bed that night, and he lived. More than twenty years later he did what he could to repay the favor by visiting the Babe as he lay dying of cancer in his New York apartment.

It was tragic that the Babe's last years were troubled by his unfulfilled desire to manage the Yankees. One day late in the 1934 season he choked down his pride long enough to ask Colonel Ruppert for the job. It was just as embarrassing for the Colonel as it was for Ruth. "Well, Babe," Ruppert said slowly, "I know you want to manage the Yankees. I know what it means to you. But it's a big job, and you don't have any experience managing. I've been thinking about it myself and I have an idea. How would you like to manage the Newark ball club for a while, and then we can see—"

The Babe hadn't expected that. He was shocked, and at first he didn't know what to say. Newark was the prize club of the whole Yankee farm system, but it was still Newark, not New York. The Babe shook his big head slowly. "I'm a big-leaguer. I've always been a big-leaguer. Let McCarthy go to Newark."

But McCarthy was Ruppert's man, so instead of ending his magnificent career happily, as he should have, Babe Ruth ended it sadly, even bitterly. He played for a while, in 1935, for the Boston Braves, but it was a mistake all around. He found himself in the middle of an unpleasant front-office situation on the Braves, and although he thought his contract gave him the right to claim the manager's job in 1936 if he wanted it, he found out that the clause he was counting on had been written by a Philadelphia lawyer and wasn't worth a nickel. About all the Babe got out of his unhappy experience in Boston before he finally quit in the middle of the season was one last great day.

It happened at Forbes Field in Pittsburgh on May 25, 1935, and for a few hours it was the old Babe Ruth out there on the ball field again. The first time up he hit a two-run homer off Red Lucas. He hit another homer in the third inning, off Guy Bush. In the fifth, with Bush still pitching, and with the crowd clamoring for him to do it again, he slugged a majestic drive over the right-field grandstand for his 714th and last regular-season home run (he also hit 15 in World Series games and one in an All-Star game for a total of 730). If, sometime in the future, another great hitter finds himself drawing close to Ruth's awesome home-run total—and I don't think it will ever happen—it's only fair that he will have to sweat hardest of all to get past the three home runs a tired old Babe Ruth hit out of Forbes Field in Pittsburgh on his last big day.

Babe did have one other day of glory, but it was a different kind, and although it was a day of warm tribute to a well-loved hero, it was also a day of sadness. That was Babe Ruth Day at Yankee Stadium, Sunday, April 27, 1947. The big crowd cheered him to the rafters of the big Stadium that, more than any other one man, he had, in a very real sense, built. He was wearing his trademarks, the camel's hair coat and the cap that matched, but he was painfully gaunt and a couple of the boys had to give him a boost up the dugout steps when he walked out onto the field to acknowledge the cheers. He was game, though, when I asked him to say a few words to the crowd. I can hear him now, the hoarse voice left to him after his throat operation croaking hesitantly. "Thank you very much, ladies and gentlemen," he said. "You know how bad my voice sounds. Well, it feels just as bad." He waited awhile to get his voice back, and he grinned a little, as if he was laughing at himself. Then he grew serious again. "The only real game, I think, in the world, is baseball." You could hardly hear his words come out of the Stadium loudspeakers, but he went on. "There's been so many nice things said about me. I'm glad I had the opportunity to thank everybody." He turned around then, a little unsteady on his feet, and walked like a soldier back to the dugout. Yogi Berra told me afterward that some of the ballplayers were wondering if they ought to jump up and take his arm. But one of the old-time baseball writers said softly, "Leave him alone. He knows where the dugout is."

Francis Cardinal Spellman, who had said a prayer to open the program, shook Babe's hand. "Good luck, Babe," he said. "I just wanted to say that any time you want me to come to your house and give you Holy Communion, I'll be glad to do it." The Babe showed the old grin. "Thanks, your Eminence," he said. "Thanks just the same, but I'd rather come down to your place."

A year later he was dead, and his body lay in state in the rotunda at Yankee Stadium until it was time for the funeral. The fans came by the thousands to say good-by to him; fathers brought their young sons and told them what it had been like to see this big fellow hit the ball out of the park, told them what he had meant to the Yankees and to baseball. At the funeral service itself, on a blazing hot August day, the pallbearers, many of them old teammates, carried the Babe's body to his last resting place. "Lord," Joe Dugan said in a whisper to Waite Hoyt, "I'd give my right arm for an ice-cold beer." "So would the Babe," Hoyt said.

It's painful to remember how tragically the careers of both the great Yankee power hitters of that time ended. Lou Gehrig was an even more impressive physical specimen than Ruth. Where the Babe was top-heavy and spindly-legged, looking less an athlete than he really was, Lou was the very model of a superbly muscled, finely trained competitor. He possessed the build of a heavyweight champion. He didn't smoke, drank little, made sure he got plenty of sleep, and was always ready to play a doubleheader without breathing hard. Except for his attractive wife, Eleanor, he had no interests outside of baseball. He was no cheap skate but he was careful of his money and was determined that he and his wife would be secure in their later years. He couldn't have been more different from Babe Ruth. Yet both of them died much too young, and Ruth lasted longer than Gehrig.

There is no explaining it. It was Gehrig, not Ruth, who was known as "The Iron Horse." It was Gehrig, not Ruth, who played in 2,130 consecutive games for the Yankees, an all-time major-league record for durability, a record that will be at least as hard to match as Ruth's 714 home runs. Unfortunately, it was a record established at heavy cost. Lou played when he was doubled over with lumbago, when he was woozy from being hit on the head by wild pitches; he even played with fractured hands. But he hung in there, and then, too soon, he was gone. He didn't have time to enjoy the center of the stage, after Ruth's departure, for more than one or two good bows. Maybe the best hour he knew was in the 1936 World Series with the Giants when the Yankees, leading two games to one, took the fourth game of the Series—and a commanding lead —on Gehrig's tremendous two-run home run off the ace of the Giants' staff, Carl Hubbell. The fans cheered him that day just as they used to cheer the Babe. "Old Biscuit Pants," as they had called him for years with affection but also with a touch of condescension, was the big man on the ball club now. But it didn't last long. Everybody could see, in 1938, that something had happened to him, and in 1939 he played only eight games before he blew the whistle on himself.

Some people are just destined to play second fiddle, and Gehrig was such a one. Who remembers that, in 1927, Lou hit 47 home runs? All anybody remembers, as Franklin P. Adams once wrote, is that "he was the guy who hit all those home runs the year Babe Ruth broke the record." Lots of people are aware that Ruth's lifetime batting average was a surprisingly high .342, but only the real students of the game remember that the Babe's partner in fence-busting, Gehrig, had a lifetime average of .340. Almost nobody knows the story Ruth always told about the day he called his home-run shot against the Cubs in the 1932 World Series. "Lou was waiting at the plate to shake hands with me," Babe said, "and I told him, 'You do the same thing, kid.' And he said, 'I will,' and he did. He hit the first pitch into the bleachers in right field. It always bothered me that nobody ever paid any attention to that."

Then, take June 3, 1932, when the Yankees were playing the old Philadelphia Athletics at Shibe Park in Philadelphia, and Lou hit four home runs in four consecutive times at bat. The Babe, in all his career, never hit four in one game, let alone four in consecutive times up, and he meant it when he told Lou after the game, "Kid, that was the greatest I ever seen." Joe McCarthy meant it, too, when he patted his big first-baseman on the back and said, "Well, Lou, nobody can ever take this away from you." Which was true enough. Except that that turned out to be the afternoon on which John McGraw, the great manager of the Giants, chose to announce his retirement from baseball. And you know who got all the head-lines on the sports pages the next day, don't you? It wasn't Lou Gehrig.

It seems bitterly unfair that if it hadn't been for his astonishing consecutive-game streak, Gehrig might have gone even more un-noticed. It would have been baseball's shame. He holds the record for the most runs batted in in World Series play, with 35. He was the American League batting champion in 1934 with .363. He led the league in runs batted in in 1927, 1930, 1931 and 1934, and he tied Ruth for the honor in 1938. Naturally, he still holds the record (12) for the most years playing 150 or more games per season. He holds the record for the most years (13) scoring 100 or more runs, the most years (7) batting in 150 or more runs, the most times (5) collecting four long hits in one game, and a few other odds and ends.

One time when he attracted the spotlight, though, was May 2, 1939, when the Yankees were at Briggs Stadium in Detroit for a game with the Tigers. Lou's famous iron-man record stood at 2,130 consecutive games. But he was in poor shape, and everybody knew it. It had started late in the season of 1938. He finished that year with a respectable .295 batting average, but he didn't hit much to-ward the end of the season. He was tired, drawn, unsure of himself.

If he didn't concentrate on what he was doing, sometimes when he picked up a coffee cup, he would drop it. There was something wrong. He thought he was just tired, and that he would be all right after a good rest over the winter. But he wasn't. It was no better in spring training, and even worse in the first eight games of the 1939 season. He managed to hit the ball safely 4 times out of 28 tries in those eight games, for a .143 average. He knew he wasn't helping the ball club, that in truth he was holding it back, and that hurt him more than anything else in the world could—including putting a stop to his cherished record.

On that morning of May 2 Lou waited in the lobby of the Book-Cadillac Hotel until he saw Joe McCarthy step out of the elevator. He walked over to him. "You'd better take me out today, Joe," he said quickly, the old cheerful smile highlighting the big dimples on his Dutch-boy's cheeks. The manager just nodded and said, "Whatever you say, Lou. It's up to you."

Later Gehrig explained it carefully to the newspapermen. "It wouldn't be fair to the boys, to Joe, to the fans, or even to me, to try going on," he said. "I decided on it Sunday night. I knew after Sunday's game that I ought to get out of there. I got up four times with men on base. Once there were two on. A hit any of those times would have won us the ball game. But I left all five men on. . . . McCarthy's been swell about it. He'd let me go until the cows came home, he's that considerate of my feelings. Well, maybe a rest will do me some good. Maybe it won't. Who knows? I'm just hoping."

As the Yankees' captain, Gehrig carried the lineup card out to the plate and handed it to the umpire in chief. The public address announcer told the crowd that Lou had decided, after 2,130 games on first base, to stand down, and as he walked back to the dugout he was followed by a deafening volley of cheers, a rising crescendo of noise that had his eyes wet as he took a place on the bench. Lefty Gomez, who had always enjoyed kidding him, sat down next to him, put his arm around Lou's broad shoulders, and said, "Hell, Lou, it took them fifteen years to get you out of the ball game. Sometimes they get me out of there in fifteen minutes."

A month later Lou left the Mayo Clinic in Rochester, Minnesota, carrying a sealed envelope containing X-ray pictures and a blunt diagnosis of his condition. With Gehrig's permission, the Mayo Clinic authorities released a statement to the press which read in part:

"He is suffering from amyotrophic lateral sclerosis. This type of illness involves the motor pathways and cells of the central nervous system, and in lay terms is known as a form of chronic poliomyelitis (infantile paralysis). The nature of this trouble makes it such that Mr. Gehrig will be unable to continue his active participation as a baseball player."

It also meant that Lou had only a couple of years to live. Whether or not Lou ever knew this is a matter of dispute. His wife, Eleanor, did everything in her power to keep it from him. So did his old friends among the ballplayers, the broadcasters and the sports-writers. Whenever Eleanor threw a party for Lou at their Riverdale, New York, home a few miles north of Yankee Stadium, all of the gang turned out, and nobody talked about the forbidden subject—including Lou. But most of his old friends think Lou knew what was going on. And, as Eleanor has said in the years since, "In his own way, he was happy."

He was happy about the fact that the Yankee ballplayers voted him a full share of their 1939 World Series money. It was probably the only time in his life that Lou ever got anything for nothing, but even that generous gesture exacted its price. It must have cost him more to sit on the bench and have the money fall into his hands than it ever did to get out there on the ball field and earn it with the sweat of his body.

Another tribute to the Iron Horse was the action of the Baseball Writers Association of America, in December, 1939, when they waived the rule that a player must be out of the game for a year before he could be voted into the Hall of Fame at Cooperstown, New York. (Now you have to be out of the game for five years.) Without waiting the required period, the writers voted Lou into the Hall of Fame right then and there. They knew how short his time was, and they wanted to do that little thing for him before he died.

Everybody wanted Lou to know, in those last few months, how much he was respected—and loved. Eleanor didn't have to worry about inviting people to come to the house; they came without being asked. Broadway and Hollywood actors and actresses, famous writers, café society celebrities, government officials and business executives, ballplayers and fighters and jockeys, cops, firemen and United States senators, they all came to the house for a few drinks and a few hours with Lou. Even in the last months they crowded into Lou's room, sat on the bed and on the floor, told funny stories, sang songs, reminisced about the great days of Murderers' Row, and did what they could to tell him—without ever really telling him— that they loved him and were going to miss him. "The house was like a circus," Eleanor Gehrig will tell you now. "But I was glad to have them all come. I would have paid them to come. I wanted to keep Lou busy, and I wanted him to have a little fun. For that matter, all the excitement kept me busy, too, and kept me from thinking too much."

Jack Sher, who has written a lot of fine movies in Hollywood in recent years, spent a good deal of time with Lou that last year doing a definitive story of his life. "During the clamor and the gayety," he remembers, "Lou would sometimes catch Eleanor's eye and his mouth would twist into the shy grin she knew so well. His eyes were calm; his face, when it wasn't showing pain, was cheerful. Eleanor was still convinced that he didn't know he was going to die, and of course, nobody ever told him that he was. But suppose he had known? Was there anything, really, that anybody could have said to him? He was not a man who knew how to put emotion into words, unless it involved something that would have helped somebody else, and he was not a man who wanted to be pitied. Except for Eleanor, he walked that last mile by himself."

By the end of May, 1941, Lou was too weak to see even his oldest friends. And it was hard for Eleanor to act as though nothing was different, as though he still had a chance. Then, on the morning of June 2 he fell into a coma, and at ten o'clock that night Lou Gehrig died.

It was a beautiful, cloudless day, the day Lou Gehrig died—perfect baseball weather. But the Stadium was empty because the Yankees were playing in Cleveland, losing a tough ball game to Bob Feller and the Indians, 7–5. Lou's ball club was still on the road when his body was placed on view in a New York funeral home, but the kids who had loved him came by the thousands to see him. Babe Ruth came, too, driving up in a big, black limousine to say good-by to the big Dutchman who had batted behind him. The Yankees would win the pennant that year, and win many another pennant in the years to come, but in a very personal way they would never be quite the same again. But, just as surely, so long as the Yankees played baseball, whether their big man was Joe Di-Maggio or Yogi Berra or Mickey Mantle or Roger Maris or Tom Tresh, they would bear the stamp of Babe Ruth and Lou Gehrig.

Chapter 3

Never look back; somebody might be
gaining on you.—SATCHEL PAIGE

ONE of the baseball writers who likes to take his wife
with him to spring training every year tells a funny story about the
second time she made the trip with him. They had had a good time
the year before, setting up headquarters at the Vinoy Park Hotel in
St. Petersburg, where the Yankees and the Cardinals were training
then (this was before anybody had invented the Mets), and making
side trips from there to catch the other clubs at places like Clearwater, Tampa, Sarasota, Bradenton, Fort Myers and even Miami.
When you consider that this fellow's employer was picking up the
tab for the expedition, and that various ball clubs here and there
could be counted on to throw cocktail parties and dinner parties
and race-track parties and just plain party parties, you can believe it
that Mommy was really having a ball. They traveled from camp to
camp and from party to party with such delightful companions as
Kay and Red Smith and Lillian and Frank Graham. They went to
the races at Sunshine Park with Grantland Rice, Fred Russell, John
Lardner, Arthur Daley and Bill Heinz. They ate at places like Joe's
Stone Crab in Miami and the Columbia in Ybor City. This wouldn't

seem to be hard to take at all, but when they were halfway through
their second spring trip, Mommy complained bitterly to the head
of the house that she was being short-changed. "I've been down
here for spring training twice now," she said sadly, "and I haven't
met a ballplayer yet. All I keep meeting are sportswriters and broadcasters."

One of the fellows riding in the car grunted. "Honey," he said,
"you are way ahead of the game." He didn't mean it, of course. It
was just too good a line to pass up. Actually, everybody who works
on the baseball beat is an incurable fan. If we weren't, we would,
I'm sure, have found other work long ago. We admire certain ballplayers more than others, of course, and we root for them just as
fiercely as any fan, but we like them all and we tend to think that
one of the fringe benefits of the job is having the opportunity to get
to know the players as human beings, as individuals, and not just as
performers with numbers on their backs and rows of statistics opposite their names in the box scores. I'll treasure some of my associa-
tions with them as long as I live.

I will remember, for instance, Satchel Paige. Who could ever forget old Satch? But I don't mean just the Satchel Paige who became
a pitching legend in his own lifetime, who might have torn the
record book to shreds if he hadn't been kept out of the game for
twenty or thirty years by the color bar, who finally became an
American League rookie at the advanced age of forty-two or forty-
five or forty-seven or something like that and helped Lou Boudreau's
Cleveland Indians win the pennant in 1948. I mean the Satchel
Paige of the six-point program for staying young.

Satch laid down those six points with a straight face:

1. Avoid fried meats, which angry up the blood.
2. If your stomach disputes you, lie down and pacify it with cool
thoughts.
3. Keep the juices flowing by jangling around gently as you move.

4. Go very light on the vices, such as carrying on in mixed society. The social ramble ain't restful.

5. Avoid running at all times.

6. Don't never look back; somebody might be gaining on you.

No matter how you look at it, that's quite a hunk of philosophy. But, then, Satch was—and still is—quite a hunk of man. When the Indians signed him in '48, after he had "tried out" at Municipal Stadium in Cleveland by pitching to Boudreau for half an hour (he threw fifty pitches, Lou said, and only four of them were outside the strike zone), the *Sporting News* editor, the late J. G. Taylor Spink, put up a loud complaint. "Many well wishers of baseball," he editorialized, "emphatically fail to see eye to eye with the signing of Satchel Paige, the super-annuated Negro pitcher. To bring in a pitching rookie of Paige's age is to demean the standards of baseball in the big circuits."

"I demeaned the big circuits considerable that year," Satch says gently. "I win six and lose one." What's more, he had an earned-run average of 2.47, struck out 45 batters, made no errors in the field and even got himself two hits. Some of the sportswriters nominated him for Rookie of the Year. "I declined the honor," Satch says. "I wasn't sure which year those gentlemen had in mind."

Satch, who has been everywhere and done everything, is one of the greatest storytellers in baseball. I once heard him tell one about the immortal Negro League catcher and home-run hitter, Josh Gibson. "We [meaning the Pittsburgh Crawfords] was playin' the Homestead Grays in the city of Pitchburg," Satch said in his own easygoing dialect. "Josh comes up in the last of the ninth with a man on and us one run behind. Well, he hits a home run, right out of sight. Nobody ever even saw the ball come down. We waited and waited for the empire to call it a home run, or at least call it somethin', and finally he decided it ain't comin' down, so he says we win. Well, the next day we are playin' the Grays again, this time in the city of Phillydelphia, and the game is just startin' when this ball comes flyin' out of nowhere in the sky right into the Grays' center fielder's glove. Well, sir, the empire makes the call as quick as a flash. He whips off his mask and yells at Josh, who is sittin' in the dugout, 'Boy, you are out—I mean yesterday, in the city of Pitchburg!' "

Another pitcher who was as funny as he was good was Louis Norman Newsom, better known as Bobo. It would be hard to find a pitcher who worked for more different clubs than Bobo did. He started out with the Brooklyn Dodgers in the National League in 1939, winning none and losing three, and he finished up with the New York Giants in the National League in 1948, winning none and losing four. In between he pitched for the Chicago Cubs (and the Dodgers again) of the National League and for just about every club in the American League—the St. Louis Browns, the Washington Senators, the Boston Red Sox, the Detroit Tigers, the Philadelphia Athletics, and even, briefly, the New York Yankees. He missed only the Indians and the White Sox. He won over 200 major-league ball games, and if they often laughed with him when he was holding court in the bar car telling jokes on the long train rides, they never laughed at him when he was out on the mound. Well, hardly ever, anyway. They did laugh at him once, during the opening game of the 1936 season in the Washington ball park. President Franklin Delano Roosevelt had thrown out the first ball and was enjoying the ball game from his box seat as Newsom worked for the Senators against the Yankees. In the top half of the second inning, Ossie Bluege raced in from third to field a Yankee bunt. Bobo took advantage of the brief respite in his labors to look around the stands, spot the President, grin at a couple of his buddies in the press box, and just sort of count the house. As he stood there in what Babe Ruth once described as "a transom," Bluege's bullet throw to first caught him flush on the back of the head, just behind his right ear. Bobo didn't go down, he kept his feet, but he staggered like a drunken sailor for a full minute. He looked a little like Floyd

Patterson after Sonny Liston clobbered him in their first fight. Then, with a proud glance in the direction of the President, he went back to work and shut out the Yankees on four hits. In his time, Bobo had broken his collarbone, his leg, and half a dozen other joints, but Ossie Bluege had finally found the one Newsom bone that wouldn't crack—his skull.

I've always cherished a couple of favorite Newsomisms. In 1940, Bobo's best year in the majors, when he won 21 games for the Tigers and lost only 5, the late Commissioner Landis declared 91 of Detroit's farm-club players free agents on the ground that they had been "covered up," illegally held back from promotion to higher-classification leagues. The decision was a body blow to the Tigers' general manager, Jack Zeller, and Zeller wasn't in the best of humor when Newsom went into a tailspin in the 1941 season and won only 12 games and lost 20. He sent Bobo a contract calling for a lot less money in 1942 and was indignant when Newsom refused to have anything to do with it. "You've got some nerve complaining about a pay cut after you lost twenty games," Zeller told Bobo. But Bobo wasn't going to take that lying down. "I only lost twenty ball games," he came back strongly, "but you lost ninety-one ball-players." A week or so later he sent the general manager a package containing a knife, a loaf of bread and a chunk of cheese. "I send you the bread and the knife so you can practice slicing before you take up the matter of my contract again," he wrote. "The piece of cheese expresses my personal opinion of you."

Bobo was in his prime when he pitched for the Tigers in the 1940 World Series against the Cincinnati Reds. His whole family, wife, father, stepmother and sisters, had come up from Hartsville, South Carolina, to see him play. He did all right for them, too, beating Paul Derringer and the Reds 7–2 in the opening game. Then, early the next morning, his father had a heart attack in his hotel room and died. Bobo truly loved his father and he was a bitterly saddened man. But when the rest of the family went home the next day to bury his father, he decided to stay and finish out the Series. On the day of the fifth game, in Detroit, he announced that he was ready to pitch and that he was going to win this one for his old daddy. He did, too. He pitched a three-hit shutout, and you can't do much better than that. He didn't let a single Cincinnati base runner get as far as third base, and he struck out seven. It was a great performance, and the newspapers ate it up. Two days later Bobo was ready to pitch again, in the seventh and last game of the Series. He was approached by a reporter in the clubhouse, who asked him if he intended to win this one for his daddy, too. Bobo was busy oiling his glove and he barely looked up. "Why, no," he said carefully. "No, I think I'll win this one for old Bobo."

One of my all-time favorites on the roll of American League superstars is Hank Greenberg. Maybe it's because, like Lou Gehrig, he wasn't any part of a natural-born ballplayer and had to work like a horse for everything he ever got out of the game. Maybe it's because he has never taken himself too seriously. I remember Hank telling a story about a War Bond game he played while he was in the service in World War II. "Of course, I was badly out of practice," he said, "and the first time up I hit into a double play. The second time, I struck out. A friend of mine had his little girl with him in the stands, and when I struck out she applauded as hard as she could. My friend thought that was pretty rude of her and he said so. 'Why,' he wanted to know, 'can't you wait until Hank does something good and then applaud?' And the little girl said, 'Well, he did do something good. That time he only made one out.' "

It takes a man who doesn't take himself too seriously to be willing to recite the poem that Edgar A. Guest wrote about Hank back at the time the Detroit Tigers, for whom Hank hit 306 home runs in eleven seasons, drew a bead on the American League pennant in 1934, his second year with the club. Hank hit .339 and batted in 139 runs that season, so you can imagine the fuss that was kicked up late in the year when Hank let it be known that he didn't think he ought to play ball on the Jewish high holidays, Rosh Hashonah and Yom Kippur. One writer went so far as to say, "Rosh Hashonah comes every year but the Tigers haven't won the pennant since 1909." In the end, Hank agreed to play on Rosh Hashonah but stuck to his decision not to play on the somber day of atonement, Yom Kippur. So Eddie Guest, who specialized in corny poems "from the heart," wrote this about Hank, and I think Hank and I are the only two people in the country who remember it:

The Irish didn't like it when they heard of Greenberg's fame
For they thought a good first-baseman should possess an Irish name.
And the Murphys and Mulrooneys said they'd never dreamed to see
A Jewish boy from Bronxville out where Casey used to be.
In the early days of April not a Dugan tipped his hat
Or prayed to see a double when Hank Greenberg came to bat.

In July the Irish wondered where he'd ever learned to play.
"He makes me think of Casey!" Old Man Murphy dared to say.
And with fifty seven doubles and a score of homers made,
The respect they had for Greenberg was being openly displayed.
But upon the Jewish New Year when Hank Greenberg came to bat
And made two homers off pitcher Rhodes—they cheered like mad for that.

Came Yom Kippur—holy fast day world-wide over to the Jew—
And Hank Greenberg to his teaching and the old tradition true
Spent the day among his people, and he didn't come to play.
Said Murphy to Mulrooney, "We shall lose the game today!
We shall miss him on the infield and shall miss him at the bat,
But he's true to his religion—and I honor him for that!"

The only thing wrong with the poem, unless you want to be literary about it, is that Hank didn't come from Bronxville, which is a rich suburb of New York deep in the heart of Westchester County, where the millionaires live. Hank came from the Bronx, land of the apartment house, the Grand Concourse, and Yankee Stadium—and many a home run he struck against the Yankees there. The Yankees knew about him, and had him scouted by their

top man, Paul Krichell, while he played first base for the Bay Park-
ways, a fast semipro club in Brooklyn which used to draw big
crowds every Sunday in the days before television. But Hank refused to sign with the Yankees because he thought Lou Gehrig
would be playing first base for them forever. It was a big break
for the Tigers. Hank was named the Most Valuable Player in the
American League twice, and once, in 1938, he hit 58 home runs to
come within a whisper of tying Babe Ruth's record of 60. He was a
great ballplayer.

Maybe the most dramatic home run Hank ever hit, and one of
the most dramatic anybody ever hit, was the one that won the 1945
pennant for the Tigers. It was September 30, 1945, the last day
of the season. The Tigers were assured of no worse than a tie with
the Washington Senators for the pennant, but they needed one
more victory to take it all. On a rain-soaked field, with the game
starting an hour late, they took on the defending champion St.
Louis Browns, still a tough ball club. The Tigers got away in front
but the Browns tied the score, 2–2, in the seventh and took a 3–2
lead in the eighth. That's the way it stood when the Tigers came
to bat in the ninth. Hub Walker pinch-hit for the pitcher, Hal New-
houser, and clubbed a single off Nelson Potter. Skeeter Webb
bunted to first base, and when George McQuinn tried to get the lead
man at second, all hands were safe. Jack Mayo sacrificed the runners
along, manager Luke Sewell of the Browns decided to walk Doc
Cramer intentionally, and the bases were loaded for Hank Greenberg.

The game of baseball can't offer anything more than this—the
pennant hanging in the balance, the game up for grabs in the ninth
inning, the bases loaded, and the big slugger digging in at the plate.
Hank stood there calmly, a big man, a menacing man, and aimed
his bat with slow, careful strokes. The ball park subsided into that
strange, pregnant rumble which is halfway between a whisper and
a roar. Then Potter made his pitch and Greenberg took his cut. The

ball was smashed cleanly off the fat part of Hank's bat, pounded high and far in a deep, curving arc. As it began to drop in its flight, and it became apparent that it was going to fall out of reach of the straining fielder, the tumult began; when the ball actually dropped into the left-field seats all hell broke loose. There was Walker coming home, and Skeeter Webb behind him, and Cramer racing in. And there was big Hank Greenberg, the old captain just back from four years in the Army Air Force, rounding third and running hard down the line to home plate. Hank was making it known that the war was over and the men were taking the game back from the boys.

No wonder that, a few years after Hank married Caral Gimbel, the daughter of department store owner Bernard Gimbel, Mrs. Gimbel found herself being asked excitedly by a lady to whom she had just been introduced, "Oh, Mrs. Gimbel, aren't you the one who's related to Hank Greenberg?"

Then there was Ted Williams. If you try to rate the three top players of their time, you have to go with Joe DiMaggio, Stan Musial and Williams. Ted occasionally had his troubles with the press and the fans but nobody ever could fault him seriously either as a ballplayer or as a man. He was a .400 batter, in my book, both personally and professionally.

Ted's troubles, both real and imaginary, started when he was a a young ballplayer. He didn't think the fans, the writers or the broadcasters had any right to criticize him. He especially resented any criticism of his personal life or behavior. He didn't even take very kindly to any criticism offered him by his first manager, Joe Cronin, the good-natured Irishman who is now the president of the American League. Joe yanked him from ball games at least three times in his first couple of seasons for offenses like failing to run out an infield hit, loafing after fly balls and swinging halfheartedly at pitches when he was in one of his tizzies. The Boston *Record* once ran a letter from a fan saying, "Williams, the all-time, all-

American adolescent, will never wear a necktie, unless he wears it to bed. He'll never tip his cap to the guys who pay his overstuffed salary. He'll never bunt, steal, hustle, or take a sign . . . unless it suits his own royal convenience. In short, he'll continue to be just what he's always been—the prize heel ever to wear a Boston uniform."

Maybe it all happened because Ted picked up a reputation as a wise guy before he ever checked in at a Red Sox spring training camp. Before he reported for the first time in the spring of 1938 he ran into one of his future teammates, Bobby Doerr, whom he had known in the Pacific Coast League. Doerr, who had finished out the 1937 season with the Red Sox, gave Ted a quick rundown of the ball club. "Wait till you see this man Foxx hit!" he said with particular enthusiasm. And quick as a flash Ted said, "Wait till Foxx sees Williams hit!" He may have been kidding, but the story got around and it didn't do Ted any good.

One story that was told a lot back around 1948 concerned a day when the Red Sox were playing the Athletics in Philadelphia. Hardly anybody in Philadelphia had ever heard of Kansas City then. The first Boston ballplayers to run out on the Shibe Park diamond were Dominic DiMaggio, Bobby Doerr and Johnny Pesky, who some fifteen years later became the manager of the club. They were greeted by a friendly chorus of cheers. Then Williams climbed up the dugout steps and the stands shook with a sincere chorus of boos. "That," said a Red Sox player sitting on the bench, "is an excellent example of the early worm getting the bird."

But no matter how many troubles he had with the fans, the press, or even the other Red Sox ballplayers, Ted didn't have much trouble hitting the ball. In his first year up, 1939, he hit .327, hit 31 home runs and had the astonishing total of 145 runs batted in. He hit .344 in 1940 and then captured the imagination of the fans all over the league with his .406 batting average in 1941. It was an unlucky break for Ted that he picked that year to go over .400, the first time since Bill Terry's .401 in 1930 that any major-league hitter had accomplished the feat. Because 1941 was the year Joe DiMaggio hit safely in 56 straight games, and DiMaggio took the play away from Williams—even to the extent of lifting the Most Valuable Player award right out from under Ted's nose. Later on, Ted won the MVP in 1946 and 1949, and he lost it to DiMaggio in 1947 by only one point. I've always liked what Ted said when a reporter asked him if he thought that one-point loss to the Yankee center fielder was unjust. "It took DiMaggio to beat me, didn't it?" Ted said. It was a generous thing for him to say, and very typical of the professional Ted Williams—and the man as well.

The greatest sportswriter of them all, Grantland Rice, never believed what some of his colleagues wrote about Williams. Granny thought Ted was a complex, moody kid who needed a little mature understanding and seldom got it. Granny used to tell about the 1946 World Series between the Red Sox and the Cardinals, in which Ted was pretty well handcuffed. He had only five hits in twenty-five times at bat in the first six games. The Cardinals were using the "Boudreau Shift" against him, stacking the defense on the right side of the ball field and virtually conceding to Ted the left side of the diamond. He might have frustrated this unnatural setup, conceived by Lou Boudreau, then managing the Cleveland Indians, by bunting down the third-base line or chopping the ball into the wide-open spaces in left field. But instead, proud and angry, he tried to knock the ball out of the park, which was exactly what the Cardinals were hoping he would try to do. He got nowhere fast.

The night before the seventh game, a man who knew Ted pretty well and thought they were good friends went looking for him in his hotel room. The room was dark but the door was partly open and the man peeked in. He could see Ted sitting motionless by the open window. He knocked, but Ted didn't even turn his head. Downstairs, the man told Granny about it. "It kind of scared me," he said. "I figured I'd better leave him alone." But Granny didn't see it that way. He called Ted on the telephone. "What are you doing?" he demanded. "Nothing," Ted said. "I'm just lying down." "Well, get up and put on your coat, sucker," Granny said. "We're going out." And out they went, to a steak house in South St. Louis for a good dinner and a couple of hours of free and easy baseball shop talk with no strain at all. Unfortunately, that was a Ted Williams only a few baseball people were privileged to know.

I like to remember him batting with that marvelously fluid swing of his and driving his bullet shots to the far corners of the outfield; I like to remember him saying things like "I don't know what I keep playing this game for; I'd a lot rather be a fireman"; and I like to remember things like the time he slipped out through the left-field scoreboard at Fenway Park between innings of a regular season ball game and, in full uniform, gobbled down a dish of vanilla ice cream at a restaurant across the street before running back to the ball park. Not even Babe Ruth ever did that.

One of the men who did as much as anybody else to irritate Ted Williams' easily irritated temper was the inventor of the defensive shift employed so effectively against him—Lou Boudreau. There has been, in my memory, no more interesting personality or more admirable person in the game in the time I've been in it. Lou was born and still lives in Harvey, Illinois, a suburb of Chicago not far outside the big city on the Illinois Central line. His father was a good semipro ballplayer, a third baseman, and when Lou was a little boy he used to go along with him on Sunday afternoons to games in places like Momence, Chicago Heights and Kankakee. Evenings, after work, Louis Boudreau, who made his living as a machinist, would go out to the empty lot on the corner of their block and amuse himself and young Louie by hitting grounders to him. Even after he and his wife, Birdie, were divorced, Lou's father liked to play ball with his youngest son whenever he could. He drilled him by the hour in hitting, fielding and throwing, and there wasn't a kid in the neighborhood who was quicker of hand on a ball field than Louie Boudreau.

"Dad and I had a game we played with each other out on the lots," Lou says. "He would hit a hundred ground balls to me, one right after the other, and the idea was for me to see how many of them I could field cleanly before I made an error. He kept score, and each time we went out to play he would keep after me to try to break my old record. He was a tough scorekeeper, too; he didn't give me any of the doubtful ones. But he sure taught me how to go to my left and to my right, how to backhand the ball when it was the only way to stop it, and how to charge the slow ones and get my throw off before it was too late."

Lou was a natural in basketball, too, and Harvey, like almost all of the towns and cities in Illinois, was and is a basketball-minded community. Living part of the time with one of his aunts, part of the time with his mother and her second husband, and part of the time with his father in the furnished room he had taken for himself, Lou understandably felt more at home on the basketball court or the ball field than he did anywhere else. He worked hard to improve himself, and succeeded so well that by the time he got to high school he was obviously far out of the ordinary. His high school didn't have a baseball team, so he had to do his baseball playing on the sandlots with teams like the one from the Magic Chef stove company, the North Harvey Merchants, the Midlothian Boosters, the American Legion Post No. 155, and the Grove Street Colts of Blue Island, which is not an island but a town near Harvey. Basketball was the biggest thing in the high school sports program, and Lou automatically became a big man in the school when he made the varsity as a freshman. That was in the season of 1931–32. A year later, in March, 1933, when Lou was a sophomore, the Harvey kids won the state championship. In Illinois sports that's like winning the World Series. The people of the state love the Chicago Cubs and the Chicago White Sox, thousands of them root their heads off for the University of Illinois and other thousands go hoarse hollering for Northwestern, but the thing that binds them all together in every town and hamlet is their unrestrained enthusiasm for high school basketball. When the Harvey kids won the state tournament, they were heroes—and the most heroic figure of them all was Lou Boudreau, the playmaker of the team. Lou made All-State forward for three years in a row, and everybody in Harvey was bursting with pride in him, more so when he won a scholarship to the University of Illinois. Then, after an enormously successful sophomore season on the Illinois basketball and baseball teams, Lou was signed secretly to a contract calling for him to report after graduation to the Cleveland Indians.

The Indians promised to pay Lou a total of $5,000 for agreeing at that early date to play his big-league baseball for them. They would pay, upon the signing of the contract by Lou and his mother, $1,000 in cash. Lou specified that this should be divided equally between his mother and father. The club would then pay $100 a month to his mother as long as he remained in college. An additional $2,200 would be paid as soon as he was able to prove he was good enough to stay with the Indians for thirty days of any championship season. Out of the whole $5,000, nothing except the last $2,200 would be paid directly to Lou. This way, he hoped to accomplish two things important to him—first, to provide some financial support for his mother (and a small windfall for his father) and, second, to protect his athletic eligibility during the two years he would still be an undergraduate at the university.

All seemed right with Lou's world when his junior basketball season got under way. He had been elected captain of the team, the first junior ever so honored at Illinois, and when he led the Illini on their first invasion of New York's famous Madison Square Garden, he had the satisfaction of playing a major part in a surprise victory. Lou still has in his scrapbook a clipping from the New York *Daily News* which says this about the game:

"A veritable basketball hurricane hit the Garden last night as a streamlined Illinois University quintet headed by a positively brilliant little Frenchman named Lou Boudreau wrecked St. John's

University's unbeaten record, 60–45, in the feature of the season's opening twin bill before 14,933 pop-eyed fans. No superlatives could fittingly describe the all-around brilliance of Boudreau as he led the Big Ten co-champions to the highest scoring triumph in four seasons of collegiate basketball at the Garden. He scored nine points from all parts of the court, set up countless plays in breath-taking fashion, and gave an exhibition of dribbling that brought back memories of Mac Kinsbrunner, rated as one of the best sleight-of-hand men in the game when he played with the old St. John's Wonder Five."

Then the roof fell in on Lou. Right after the Christmas holidays he was called to the office of the athletic director and told that the Commissioner of the Western Conference—generally known as the Big Ten—had received an anonymous letter charging that he had signed a contract with the Cleveland Indians, that the Indians had already paid over a thousand dollars on the contract, and that Boudreau therefore was a professional and ineligible to compete in college athletics. Lou told the school officials exactly what had been done, pointed out that he had accepted no money himself, and left it up to them. The Athletic Board voted on the matter and split down the middle, three men voting for Lou's right to continue with the university teams and three opposed. The decision then was referred to the entire Conference, which declared him ineligible for the remainder of his junior year but ruled that if he severed all connection with the Cleveland Baseball Club he might rejoin his school teams in his senior year. Lou thought it over and decided to go along with the ruling. Then, three weeks after handing down its original decision, the Big Ten suddenly reversed it. Boudreau, they said, would not be eligible for reinstatement in his senior year.

Disgusted, and unwilling to sit out two whole years without sports competition, Lou made up his mind that he would finish out his junior year classes, then report to the Indians and begin his professional baseball career. He could return to Illinois at the end of the baseball season, do one semester's work, and then return again at the end of the next season, earn out his last semester's credits, and graduate. It was the closest he could come to having his cake and eating it; it meant a lot of hard work, but it could be done—and Lou did it.

Boudreau hit .290 at third base for Cedar Rapids of the Three-Eye League in 1938. In 1939 he hit .331 and played shortstop for Buffalo of the International League, and finished out the season hitting .258 for the Indians in 53 American League games. The Indians never had a doubt in the world that he would make it, and their faith was justified. He came close to hitting .300 for them in over ten major-league seasons and he gave them some of the finest shortstopping ever seen in the American League. Only Phil Rizzuto of the Yankees ever is rated above Boudreau as a modern-day American League shortstop, and many a fan, especially in Cleveland and Chicago and Boston, cities where Lou always exerted a special appeal, will argue that Boudreau was the better man. He wasn't fast, and he had bad ankles that he had to tape up before every ball game, but he had an amazing sense of anticipation and he could come up with the ball every time. He had a good arm, too, and he could hit. He had one other thing going for him—he was a fighter. Lou gave it the old college try every day. He was a professional, and he played baseball for money, but that wasn't what drove him once he ran out onto the diamond. As Leo Durocher likes to say, he came to play and he came to beat you.

He had ambition, too. When the Cleveland club was looking around for a new manager at the end of the 1941 season, with manager Roger Peckinpaugh moving into the front office, Lou picked up the telephone at home one day and called general manager Alva Bradley and applied for the job. He was twenty-four years old and a veteran of two and a half major-league seasons. His appointment shocked the Cleveland baseball writers, one of whom summed up the general feeling this way: "Great! They get a Baby

Snooks for a manager and at the same time they ruin the best shortstop in baseball." But Lou went on to manage the Indians through
eight seasons, and to play a great game of shortstop for them.

The thing I will always remember Boudreau for best is the play-
off game between the Indians and the Red Sox for the championship
of the American League in 1948. It had been a tough season for the
Indians all the way, up one week and down the next, and when the
154th game had been played, there they were in a flatfooted tie with
the Red Sox for first place. The toss of a coin settled the play-off
site, and the Indians had to take a train ride to Boston for the one
ball game that would settle it all. The Boston Braves, who hadn't
moved to Milwaukee yet, already had won the National League
pennant, and Lou told his ballplayers, "We're just going to Boston
one day ahead of time, that's all. We'll be ready for the Braves the
day after tomorrow."

Joe McCarthy, in his first season as manager of the Red Sox after
his long and illustrious career with the Yankees, started Denny
Galehouse. Boudreau went with his big left-handed winner, Gene
Bearden. He had talked over the pitching choice with his players in
the clubhouse after the last regular game, and Joe Gordon, acting as
spokesman for all, had said, "We've gone with your selections all
year, Lou. There's no sense changing now." So Lou picked Bearden
and sent Bob Feller and Bob Lemon out to the bullpen. The game
was on, and if there ever was a case of winner take all, this was it.

The third man up in the top of the first was Boudreau. Dale
Mitchell and Allie Clark had already made out. Lou hit a home run
over the left-field wall to make the score 1–0. The Red Sox tied the
score in their half of the inning and then there was no more scoring
until the fourth. Boudreau led off that inning for Cleveland with a
single to left. Joe Gordon also singled and Kenny Keltner hit a
three-run home run. Larry Doby, working his way around after
hitting a double, made it 5–1, and then, in the fifth, Boudreau hit
another homer. His fourth time up, in the ninth, Lou hit a single

for a perfect day at the plate in the biggest game of his life. He
finished the season with a batting average of .355. "The greatest
quarterback I ever saw on a baseball field," Frankie Frisch said of
him. And Red Smith asked in his newspaper column the next morning, "Could Connie Mack or John McGraw do a better job of managing than Boudreau did yesterday?"

It would be hard to see how anybody could. Going 4-for-4 beats
thinking any day.

Boudreau was one kind of ballplayer. Willie Mays is another.
Willie doesn't have to stop to think; he does everything by instinct.
That's the way it has been since he first came up to the Giants, a
.477 hitter at Minneapolis in the American Association, in May of
1951. He joined the ball club for a series in Philadelphia and
promptly went 0-for-13, but then the Giants moved on to the Polo
Grounds in New York and Willie hit a home run in his first game
in the old ball park—and everything has been coming up roses for
him ever since.

It was for Willie that Leo Durocher, his first manager, coined the
phrase, "He comes to play." It is around his unflagging enthusiasm
for the game that the whole Willie Mays legend has been built. The
young Willie liked to play stickball with the kids on the Harlem
streets when he went back to his furnished room after a ball game
at the Polo Grounds. His yellow Cadillac might be parked at the
curb and his freshly shined black shoes might be picking up a thick
coating of dirt, but Willie would play stickball because it was something to do with a bat and a ball. As the old folk song says about
John Henry, the steel-drivin' man, Willie was a natural man. What
he does so well on the ball field was born in him. Willie likes to be
well paid because he has been able to think of a lot of things to do
with the money he makes, but there really is no direct connection in
his mind between the money and playing ball. He knows he is worth
a lot to the Giants and he trusts Horace Stoneham, his boss, to pay
him what he is worth. But he plays ball for fun. You don't have to

be a psychologist to appreciate that without the one there probably wouldn't be the other.

At any rate, Willie understands the difference between the joy of playing ball and the seriousness of playing ball for a living. "Mr. Stoneham is my friend," he said once. "We never argue about how much I'm gonna get paid. Whatever he says is all right with me. He's my friend." Yet, on another occasion, a reporter who had known Willie ever since his rookie days said to him, "Hey, Willie, what's this I hear about you planning to hold out for $50,000 this year?" And Willie said, with the nervous giggle that is so characteristic of him, "That Mr. Stoneham would take a gun to me if I ever asked him for $50,000." Listening to this byplay, another writer broke into the conversation to say, "Willie, you'd be just as happy playing ball for nothing, wouldn't you?" Willie didn't say anything for a minute. Then he said, shaking his head slowly, "Now, remember, if you put that in the paper, *you* said it, not *me*."

Garry Schumacher, who has been handling the Giants' publicity for a good many years, likes to tell about the day Willie returned to the ball club's spring training camp at Phoenix after two years in the Army. Garry met him at the airport, and going over to the baggage counter with him, picked up his two pieces of matched luggage. It puzzled him that one of the bags was as heavy as though it were filled with lead weights and the other as light as though it contained nothing but feathers. "Willie," Garry wanted to know, "what the hell you got in these bags, they're so different?" Willie Mays, the natural ballplayer, was honest about it. "One of them's got all my clothes in it," he said. "All's that's in the other one is my glove and my jockstrap."

As far as the Giants' fans ever have been concerned—in New York or in San Francisco—that was all he needed. "The book on Willie is murder," one scout wrote in his report to his employers. "Pitch him high and you're pitching to his power. He hits a lot of homers off high pitches. But pitch him low and you're pitching to his average. He gets a piece of the low ones most of the time and that's where he gets his singles and doubles." That doesn't leave much room for the opposing pitcher to work in, but that's Willie Mays for you.

I've always been fascinated by raw, unretouched scouting reports. I find the ones on ballplayers who didn't make it just as interesting as the ones on the players who did make it. I like to look at them just as they were written by the scout and turned in to the ball club. And it's fair to say I've never seen one that reeked quite so much of conviction as the one Hank De Berry of the Giants wrote on Willie Howard Mays, Jr., in the spring of 1951 when Willie was starting his first season in Triple-A at Minneapolis. This is what it said:

Sensational. Is the outstanding player on the Minneapolis club and probably in all the minor leagues for that matter. He is now on one of the best hitting streaks imaginable. Hits all pitches and hits to all fields. Hits the ball where it is pitched as good as any player seen in many days. Everything he does is sensational. He has made the most spectacular catches. Runs and throws with the best of them. Naturally, he has some faults, some of which are: charges low-hit balls too much, runs a bit with his head down. There have been a few times when his manager needed a rope. When he starts somewhere, he means to get there, hell bent for election. Slides hard, plays hard. He is a sensation and just about as popular with local fans as he can be—a real favorite. The Louisville pitchers knocked him down plenty but it seemed to have no effect on him at all. This player is the best prospect in America. It was a banner day for the Giants when he was signed.

Willie has hit as many as 51 home runs in a single season and is justly famous for his hitting. He is equally famous for his fielding, which makes him the exact opposite of the inept ballplayer about whom the professionals used to say, "Although he is a very poor fielder, he is also a very poor hitter." Almost every baseball man has his favorite story about Willie in the field, but I think a lot of people share mine. This was the day in 1951, his rookie season, when the Giants were playing the Dodgers at the Polo Grounds, and Mays made a long, reckless run to the deepest corner of right center field to rob Carl Furillo of a sure triple and a possible home run. Billy Cox, the Brooklyn third baseman, was on third at the time, and as soon as Willie caught the ball, Cox broke for the plate. Willie had run full-tilt across the right-field foul line after he made the catch, and it would be hard to imagine a more difficult position for a right-handed outfielder to be in with a base runner racing from third to home. But Willie pivoted violently to his left, cut loose with the ball without even the semblance of a windup, and laid it into the catcher's mitt on the fly. Cox was out on the business end of a double play that every man in the ball park said was impossible.

There were two wonderful quotes about that play after the game.

"It was the perfectest throw I ever made," Willie said, with his engaging honesty.

"Aah," Charlie Dressen said. "I'd like to see him do it again!"

So far as his hitting is concerned, nobody has ever said it better than Willie said it himself. "It's not hard," he said. "When I'm not hittin', I don't hit nobody. But when I'm hittin', I hit anybody!"

I remember one other thing he said that any young ballplayer could consider with profit. "Do big-league ballplayers work as hard in spring exhibition games as they do in the regular games?" Willie was asked one day by an old gentleman in Phoenix. "I don't know about other ballplayers," Willie said. "I only know about me." The old gentleman persisted. "Well," he asked, "do you?" Willie nodded gravely. "Yeah," he said, "I do. It don't make no difference to me what kind of a game it is, I always play it as hard as I can. That's the onliest way I know how to play ball."

Chapter 4

Joe, Joe, DiMaggio . . . We want you on
our side.—SONG LYRIC

"HE seems to be very hard to get acquainted with,"
Colonel Ruppert said about Joe DiMaggio when the young man
from San Francisco came up to the Yankees. It was an accurate sum-
mary then, and it was accurate all through Joe's long and distinguished playing career, although he has mellowed considerably and
become much more approachable in the years since his retirement.

It wasn't that Joe was stuck-up or anti-people. He was just shy,
naturally a loner. His personality suited his style of play. He performed without visible passion on the ball field but with a majestic,
stately grace that was every bit as exciting to watch as the wildest
acrobatics of a Willie Mays or a Rocky Colavito. As Jimmy Cannon,
his friend, once wrote, "Only Joe Louis matched DiMaggio for pure
athlete's dignity."

The important thing about DiMaggio is that he was a whole ballplayer. This is what makes the arguments about him and Ted
Williams and Stan Musial pointless. All three were great hitters and
the chances are most professional baseball men would vote for
Williams as the best of them with the bat. But Williams was only

an average fielder and a fair thrower, and he rarely showed any interest in fielding. He was a pretty good base runner when he wanted to be. Musial cared about everything he did, just as Di-Maggio did. He was an excellent fielder and base runner, with only one major weakness; he couldn't throw very well. Stan hurt his arm way back in the late thirties when he was pitching at Daytona Beach, Florida, and it was never the same afterward. But DiMaggio had no weakness; there was no flaw in the magnificent equipment he brought to the game. He could hit with the best of them, and with power too; he could field with the best of all time, and that includes Tris Speaker; he had a throwing arm as strong and as accurate as a rifle; he could run the bases with speed and skill; and he was thinking every minute he was on the ball field. The record books won't substantiate the claim that he was the greatest ball-player of his time—other men hit more home runs, hit for higher averages, stole more bases. But Joe was the complete ballplayer. He was the best.

Three times they elected him the Most Valuable Player in the American League. They don't do that for nothing. DiMaggio had a lifetime batting average of .329, he hit 361 home runs, hit safely in 56 consecutive games in 1941, made the All-Star game year after year, and played in ten World Series—nine times with the winning club. All you have to do, even now, is close your eyes for a second and you can see him again, drifting back under a long fly ball with that slow and marvelous certainty. Every day he was on the ball field was a good day for the Yankees.

I remember something Lou Boudreau once said about DiMaggio. Somebody had asked Lou, who was managing the Indians then, how come Joe always hit Bob Feller so consistently. "I don't know," Boudreau said, "but he sure does. I'll tell you the truth, when it comes to DiMaggio, I'd rather see some other pitcher in there for us instead of Feller. When it comes down to Feller against DiMaggio, the best against the best, Joe always gives it that little extra."

Of course he did. DiMaggio was a proud man, proud of his skills and proud of his ball club. There was a time in 1947 when he couldn't get untracked at the plate and he hung around .270 and .275 for weeks. The day he finally made it up over .300 he went out to dinner with Jimmy Cannon. They walked down Broadway for a few blocks and had to stop every couple of feet while some delighted fan who had spotted Joe—he must have one of the most recognizable faces in America—congratulated him on getting back to .300. "I better keep hitting," Joe said. "I forgot how nice this is."

It was because he was so proud that Joe quit as a player at the end of the 1951 season even though the Yankees very much wanted him to go on at least one more year and were willing to give him his fourth straight $100,000 contract. Joe quit because he knew he was not the ballplayer he had been and because he was unwilling to show the fans an imitation DiMaggio. (A year later he even quit his exceedingly lucrative job doing the postgame television show at Yankee Stadium because he didn't think he was good enough and he refused to go on taking the money if he couldn't deliver.)

There was a day in his last season when Casey Stengel took him out of his old cleanup spot as the number four hitter in the batting order and replaced him with Yogi Berra. Stengel put DiMaggio fifth. It seemed like a smart move by Casey when Yogi hit a triple in the first inning to put the Yankees ahead of the Indians, 1–0. DiMaggio, following Berra, hit a ground ball back to the pitcher, Feller. The next time up, Joe hit into a double play. Then, in the fifth inning, with a man on second and two out, Feller walked Berra intentionally. It was an unprecedented humiliation for DiMaggio, but he showed nothing but solemn interest as he knelt in the on-deck circle and watched Yogi take the four wide ones. There were men in the press box, though, old friends of his, who were appalled at this contemptuous treatment of the greatest Yankee of them all. "Come on, Joe," more than one of the usually detached reporters rooted, "knock one over the fence." In the crowd of more than

70,000, there were many who uneasily contemplated the embarrassment Joe was about to suffer and that they would suffer along with
him.

Feller's first pitch was a strike, his second a ball. Joe swung at the
next one, belatedly, hesitantly, as though he had intended to let it
go by and then had changed his mind at the last second. Now Feller,
ahead of him one ball and two strikes, came in with the pitch that
was keeping him in the league, his slider. DiMaggio swung, no hesi-
tating this time, swung with the marvelous leverage and grace
generated by his distinctive flat-footed stance, and the crack of the
bat against the ball told you it was a base hit. The ball flew on a
wicked low line, like an Arnold Palmer two-iron shot, between the
left fielder and the center fielder, and rolled unmolested to the
fence, 450 feet or more from the plate. Two runs were in when Di-
Maggio pulled up at third with his triple. He didn't even have to
slide.

But there weren't enough moments like that for him that year,
and he knew he didn't want to go through another one like it—or,
worse, one in which he might be able to produce even less. Eddie
Lopat went over to his locker after a night game in early September
and asked him to autograph a ball for him. Joe had had a pretty
good night and Eddie kidded him about it. "You were like a young
buck out there tonight," he said. Joe lifted his can of beer and
grinned. "It's the cool weather," he said. "A clean uniform, a shave
and a haircut." Joe knew he was losing it, and he didn't tolerate any
empty flattery. Facing the fact that they don't have it any more is
the hardest thing most ballplayers ever have to do, but DiMaggio
did it as easily and as gracefully as he caught a fly ball. "The old boy
can't be that bad," he said once after he had had a bad game. It
hurt him, as it hurts every great athlete, to concede that he couldn't
do it any more, but he was big enough to see it and to admit it.

I've always thought that the clincher in Joe's decision to retire
was supplied by a scouting report Andy High made up on the

Yankees for the Dodgers in 1951. When the Dodgers blew the play-off to the Giants, they didn't have any use for the report. Somehow, *Life* magazine got hold of it. It said some harsh things about Di-Maggio: "He can't stop quickly and throw hard. You can take the extra base on him if he is in motion away from the line of throw. He won't throw on questionable plays and I would challenge him even if he threw a man or so out. He can't run and won't bunt. His reflexes are very slow and he can't pull a ball at all." What hurt Joe the most was that he knew it was all true. The home run he hit to beat the Giants in the fourth game of the Series made him feel better but didn't fool him into changing his mind. It was Di-Maggio's last season and he went out a champion, which was the way he came in.

Because his first marriage had broken up and caused him a lasting hurt, all the Yankees hoped that Joe's second marriage, to Marilyn Monroe, would last forever. It was sad for Joe, and perhaps tragic for Marilyn, that it didn't. They seemed, at first look, to be an oddly assorted couple, but as became apparent after Marilyn's shock-ingly early death, Joe cared tremendously for her and gave her a limitless loyalty. She visited him a couple of times in Florida after their divorce when he had accepted Dan Topping's invitation to help coach the Yankee hitters, and the whole ball club was crazy about her. It reminded me of the time they were first married and somebody asked one of the writers who travels with our club, "Is this going to be good for DiMaggio?" The writer, who is a thought-ful type, said carefully, "It's got to be better than rooming with Joe Page."

The chances are that when future historians of the game look back on DiMaggio's career they will marvel most at his remarkable hitting streak of 1941. Fifty-six games in a row—it was a record to endure, a record made under such incredible tension that, in the streak's later stages, even the fans were nervous as they took their seats and got ready to watch Joe try to do it again. It started on May 15 against the Chicago White Sox and it lasted until July

17, the night Joe tried to make it 57. That was a night to remember. There were 67,468 people in the big Cleveland ball park, a new record crowd for a major-league night game. Since most of them were rabid Indian fans and glad to see trouble of any kind befall the Yankees, it is safe to assume that they saw what they had come to see. They saw the longest consecutive-game hitting streak in baseball history come to an end. After hitting safely in 56 straight games, first breaking George Sisler's American League record of 41 games and then catching up to and passing Willie Keeler's major-league record of 44 games set with the old Baltimore Orioles of the National League exactly 44 years before, Joe DiMaggio was finally stopped.

It took two pitchers, lefty Al Smith and right-hander Jim Bagby, Jr., and two tremendous plays by third baseman Ken Keltner of Cleveland to stop him. Joe faced Smith, the starter, three times. The first time up he smashed a hot one to Keltner, who made a fine stop and throw to get him at first. The second time he walked. The third time he hit another sizzler to Keltner, who got him again on a play that brought the crowd to its feet. The Yankees got Smith out of there in the eighth, and with the bases loaded and one out, DiMaggio batted against relief pitcher Bagby. He hit the ball sharply on the ground, right to shortstop Lou Boudreau, who was celebrating his twenty-fourth birthday that night. It was an easy double-play ball. Boudreau threw to second baseman Ray Mack to get one and Mack threw to Oscar Grimes at first for the double play. The crowd knew that DiMaggio's streak was over. It wasn't likely that Joe would get up again in the ninth, and he didn't.

Actually, Joe hit safely in 57 straight games that year because he had a hit in the All-Star game in Detroit on July 8. But that one didn't count in the records. He finished up five games short of his own career record. He had hit safely in 61 straight games in 1933 when he was playing for the San Francisco Seals in the Pacific Coast League.

The Seals produced three outfielding DiMaggios for the big

leagues. The first was Vince, who is best remembered for the frequency with which he struck out. Joe was the second. The third, and a fine ballplayer in his own right, was Dominic, center fielder for the Boston Red Sox from 1940 to 1952, a gifted defensive outfielder—many were the base hits he took away from his big brother —and a solid hitter whose lifetime batting average in the major leagues was a fine .298. Dom was a lot like Joe in personality, reserved and withdrawn, but Vince was an outgoing fellow, easy to know and easy to like. Even the monotonous regularity with which he struck out failed to squelch his good humor. Vince, who got around the National League like a traveling salesman—playing with Boston, Cincinnati, Pittsburgh, Philadelphia and New York before finally going back to San Francisco—was a born optimist. "He's the only player I ever saw who could strike out three times in one game and not be discouraged or embarrassed," said Casey Stengel, who managed him with the Boston Braves. "He'd take his three whiffs and walk into the clubhouse whistling. Everybody would be feeling sorry for him but Vince always thought he was doing good." They claim that before a Braves-Cardinals game at Boston in 1937, a St. Louis fan bet Dizzy Dean, who was pitching that day, he couldn't strike out Vince four times. "I'll bet you twenty cents a strikeout," the fan offered, and Diz took him up on it. His first three times up, Vince fanned on schedule. The fourth time, he fouled off the first pitch and then, on the second, lifted a dinky pop foul just back of the plate. Bruce Ogrodowski, the Cardinals' catcher, was going back for it, and it looked like an easy catch. But Dean rushed in from the mound shouting, "Drop it! Drop it!" Understandably flustered, Ogrodowski did exactly that. Diz patted him gratefully on the shoulder. "Good boy," he said, grinning. "I got a bet I can strike him out. You almost ruint it." Frankie Frisch was managing the Cardinals then, and it was a good thing he didn't know what was going on. He was still trying to figure it out when Dean threw his high, hard one in there for the third

strike on DiMaggio and his 80-cent profit. When Harold Kaese, the
Boston sportswriter, tells this story, he always adds that when you
consider what the Cardinals were paying Dean in those days, it's
no wonder he was so eager to make an extra 80 cents.

It's a good thing Vince DiMaggio scattered a few laughs around
the league because brother Joe didn't have time for that sort of
thing. He took his baseball seriously, and when it came to baseball
he took himself seriously, with no false modesty clouding his coldly
objective view of his own equipment. There was the time a little
crowd of interviewers and well-wishers gathered around his locker
at the Stadium after the second game of the 1947 World Series, and
one of the writers, Bob Cooke of the New York *Herald Tribune,*
brought up the subject of the troubles Pete Reiser of the Dodgers
had had in center field that afternoon. Both Gene Hermanski of
the Dodgers and Johnny Lindell of the Yankees had had a hard
time with the sun in left field, too. DiMaggio was quick to defend
the ballplayers. "The shadows are tough here in the fall," he said,
"and it's always worse when there's a big crowd and you get all that
smoke hanging over the ball field. The combination of the sun and
the shadows and the smoke is really rough."

This seemed reasonable to Cooke, but then he wondered, "What
about you, Joe? How come it doesn't bother you?"

DiMaggio didn't say anything for a moment, then he grinned
that quick, shy grin of his and said, "You aren't going to start
worrying about the old boy now, are you?"

"I realized then," Cooke said in writing about the incident, "that
Joe had been explaining about the hazards the background presented to ordinary outfielders. It never even occurred to him that
he might have trouble out there."

The only serious trouble Joe ever had in baseball was with his
physical condition. He had more than his share of injuries and ill-
nesses, beginning with the freak accident that made him miss the
first dozen or so games of his rookie season because of a badly

burned foot suffered during a diathermy treatment at the St. Petersburg training camp. His worst siege was with the famous bone spur he developed in his right heel. The spur was the result of a calcium deposit developed during the 1948 season, most of which Joe played under the handicap of persistent and debilitating pain. An operation had been performed on the heel at Johns Hopkins Hospital in Baltimore in November, 1948, and Joe had hoped he would be all set for the season of 1949. The first indication he had that he might be in for more trouble came during the early stages of the training season in Florida. The heel hurt when he ran; it hurt the same way it had hurt the year before. Understandably disturbed, Joe flew back to Baltimore to see the doctors who had operated on him. They checked him carefully, took new X rays, and told Joe firmly that the spur was not growing back, as he feared it was. But when Joe flew back to St. Petersburg and put on his uniform again, the heel still hurt. DiMaggio wouldn't have minded the pain if he had felt sure that it was only temporary and that the condition that caused it was healing. But he was convinced that it wasn't temporary and it wasn't healing. For the first time since he had come up to the Yankees in 1936, he began to think he was through. Finished. Washed up as a ballplayer. It wasn't a pleasant thing to think about. Always a loner, Joe really shut himself off from the world. Georgie Solotaire, the Broadway ticket broker, and Toots Shor, his two closest friends, were the only two people who saw him at all when he returned alone to New York after taking more treatments in Baltimore. He just stayed locked up in his room at the Hotel Madison on 58th Street, killing time and brooding.

Then, without any warning, one morning when he got out of bed and, out of long habit, put his heel gently down on the floor, it suddenly struck him that it didn't hurt. It had been hurting for so long that he could hardly believe it. But he walked around the room a dozen times or more, hardly daring to credit the way he felt, and

there was no pain at all. In another day he was up at Yankee
Stadium taking the uniform with number 5 on the back out of
the corner locker next to the doorway into the trainer's room. He
took batting practice until his hands were blistered, and the heel
still didn't hurt. That was good enough for Joe. He was happy
again. He talked to Casey Stengel and told the manager that he
thought it would be a good idea to test the heel in a game that didn't
matter, like the exhibition game coming up with the Giants for the
benefit of the city's Sandlot Baseball Fund. So Casey put him in
the lineup, thinking that the big fellow might go for a few
innings if all went well—and praying that it would. It was a hard
thing for old Case, in his first year as manager of the Yankees, to
have the greatest ballplayer in the game on his side but not able
to play. He was too smart to hurry things along but he was only
human and he was hoping.

It surprised DiMag as much as anybody else that he played the
whole nine innings of that exhibition game and then went along
with the ball club for a three-game series in Boston. The opener,
Joe's first league game of the season, was a night game on June 28.
Even the Boston fans gave him a big hand when he came up for the
first time. He didn't do anything then, but the next time up, in the
third inning, with Phil Rizzuto on base ahead of him, Joe put one
in the seats. No wonder he felt good after the game, sitting in front
of his locker in his undershirt, slowly drinking a cold can of beer.

"How do you do it?" one of the Boston newspapermen asked
him. "I hear you only worked out a half a dozen times, and then
that one exhibition game, and now this. Come on, how do you do
it, Joe?"

DiMaggio grinned. "You just go up there and swing at the ball,"
he said. "There's no skill involved."

Maybe not, but it didn't look like any accident in the next
game when he picked up right where he had left off. The Yankees
were losing that one, 7–1, when Joe came to bat in the top of the

fifth with two men on. Joe hit one over the left-field screen and it was 7–4. Gene Woodling tied it up in the seventh when he hit a double with the bases loaded, and then Joe won the ball game with another home run in the eighth.

If you were a writer making up a story about a great hitter, you wouldn't have the nerve to pile more heroics on top of what Joe had already done in one series. But Joe wasn't worrying about people believing him. The Yankees were trying to hold on to a 3–2 lead in the seventh inning of the third game when George Stirnweiss and Tommy Henrich hit singles back to back. That brought Joe up, and you could hardly hear yourself think, there was so much noise in Fenway Park. Mel Parnell pitched to him carefully, trying not to give him anything too good to hit, but when the count went to 3-and-2, Parnell had to come in with the ball and Joe tagged it for a home run that won the game. He finished the series with five hits, four of them home runs. He was an old man as ballplayers go, and he hadn't been in a game all year. But he was still Joe DiMaggio. The next week, *Life* put him on the cover and paid him something like $5,000 for his own story of his comeback.

For two months DiMaggio played great ball, and along with Henrich and Berra carried the Yanks toward another pennant. Then, in September, he came down with virus pneumonia, and for a while things didn't look good for either him or the Yanks. The Red Sox came to New York for a two-game series on the last two days of the season, leading the Yankees by a game. With only those two games left to play, all the Red Sox, who were being managed then by old Mr. Yankee himself, Joe McCarthy, had to do was win one of them and they were in. But they couldn't do it. Johnny Lindell's home run helped the Yankees win the first game, on what had long been scheduled as Joe DiMaggio Day, and Tommy Henrich's homer and Jerry Coleman's bases-loaded double in the eighth inning broke up the deciding game and gave the Yankees the pen-

nant. I remember Tommy saying afterward, "I had to do it. I hit
a home run in the first game of the season and I just had to hit one
in the last game. I was sure I was going to do it. Bill Dickey told
me I would."

The first of those two all-or-nothing games with the Red Sox
was one of the high points of Joe DiMaggio's career. He had been
confined to his bed for two weeks; the virus siege had left him a
good ten pounds under his usual weight and he looked tired and
haggard. But he stood out on the infield for a full hour before the
game while 69,551 idolatrous Yankee fans celebrated Joe DiMaggio Day with him. I had the pleasure of serving as master of ceremonies for the occasion and it was a memorable experience. Neither
I nor anybody else who was there will ever forget Joe, standing
at home plate, trying to keep the emotion out of his eyes and out
of his voice, and saying, "I'd like to thank the good Lord for making me a Yankee."

Characteristically, Joe started out by saying, "I'd like to apolo-
gize to the people in the bleachers for having my back turned to
them." And he didn't mind admitting, "This is one of the few
times I've choked up. Many years ago Lefty O'Doul told me, 'Joe,
don't let the big town scare you. New York is the most generous
town in the world.' This day proves it.

"I've played for three managers and they all taught me something. If we don't win I will say to McCarthy, 'If we couldn't win,
I'm glad you did.' The Red Sox are a grand bunch of guys. But that
doesn't include the guy out in center field who spends so much
time annoying me."

At that point the fellow he was talking about, Joe's brother
Dominic, walked out of the visitors' dugout to stand next to him,
along with their mother—who knew she was going to have one
son in the World Series no matter which team won these two games
—and little Joe Jr. They heard Mayor Bill O'Dwyer tell DiMaggio,
"You came here from San Francisco. After today you will never

leave New York." And they heard Dan Daniel of the New York *World-Telegram,* speaking for all the baseball writers, say, "Joe came to St. Petersburg wearing a size 7¼ hat, and he still wears the same size. He is the player's player, the manager's player, the fan's player, the player of the writers who have been with him and the Yankees for many years."

Joe McCarthy got a tremendous hand when he came out to congratulate the man who had helped him win six pennants. (DiMaggio was in the army when McCarthy won his seventh in 1943.) Ethel Merman sang "Take Me Out to the Ball Game." Then it was time for Joe's gifts—and what a procession of them there was. A lot of cash had been donated for the occasion, and all of that was, at DiMaggio's insistence, turned over to the Damon Runyon Cancer Fund and the Heart Fund. A four-year college scholarship had been set up for a boy to be selected by Joe. Then there was a Cadillac for Joe, a nifty Dodge for his mother, a beautiful Chris-Craft speedboat, two television sets, all kinds of personal jewelry, a couple of rifles, a living-room carpet and the inevitable wacky items that always are good for a laugh at such presentations—a case of shoestring potatoes, a cocker spaniel, a baseball and bat made out of Christmas candy, a set of electric trains for little Joe, and a case of frozen lima beans.

All this, and the Yankees won the ball game too. When they locked up the pennant the next day, Joe DiMaggio must have been one of the most contented men in the world. He had every right to be. If it hadn't been for him, the man they had said was through, the Yankees could never have done it.

There wasn't much time left for Joe after that, but there were two more pennants and two more world championships—a clean sweep of the Philadelphia Phillies in 1950 and then a six-game trouncing of the Giants in 1951 when a nineteen-year-old rookie named Mickey Mantle made his first World Series appearance for the Yankees—the first of many. In Joe's last World Series game he set a new record for the most Series games ever played by one man. The record had been Frank Frisch's, with 50. The sixth game of the 1951 Series made it 51 for DiMaggio. (A record which Yogi Berra left far behind before he hung up his spikes.)

But it had to end sometime, and it finally did end at two o'clock on the afternoon of December 11, 1951. The Yankees called a press conference at that hour in their offices in the Squibb Building at 745 Fifth Avenue in New York, and to the surprise of very few, if any, people close to the game, Joe DiMaggio walked into the room and announced that he was retiring. "Del Webb and I worked on Joe until ten o'clock last night," Dan Topping said, "but he wouldn't change his mind." Dan admitted that they had offered Joe a contract for $100,000, the same amount he had been paid from 1949 through 1951. It made no difference.

"I told you fellows last spring I thought this would be my last year," DiMaggio told the reporters. "I only wish I could have had a better year. But even if I had hit .350, this would have been the last year for me. . . . Old injuries caught up with me and brought on new ones. I found that it was hard for me to straighten up after I picked up a ground ball. . . . All the fun had gone out of playing the game."

The writers, told that Joe was going to do the pregame and postgame television shows at Yankee Stadium for the 1952 season, asked him if he had any thoughts of becoming a major-league manager. He said no. "The fact is," he said, "I don't want to put on a baseball uniform again at all, and I certainly don't want to have to worry about twenty-five other men."

I think for the few hours that press conference lasted Joe thought retiring was going to be tougher than playing. The club had setups in four different rooms, one for the reporters, one for the radiomen, one for the television and newsreel cameramen, and one for the still photographers. Joe had to go from one room to another, trying to satisfy the requests of all, and he worked up a pretty good sweat before it was all wrapped up. There were so many people there that the caterers had to replenish the supplies of sandwiches, coffee and cheesecake three times.

I can still see Joe standing there in front of a big photographic mural of himself as a young man swinging a bat, and I can still hear him saying, "I've played my last game of ball."

Bill Corum, who's gone now, said it for all of us: "Good luck, Joe. You were a big man in our town and you always will be."

Chapter 5

It ain't nothin' till I call it.—BILL KLEM

THERE must be a hundred Bill Klem stories, but my favorite about the greatest umpire of them all is the one about Bill's advice to the rookie pitcher working against Stan Musial in a spring exhibition game at the end of World War II. The young pitcher resented Bill's call of ball one on his first pitch. He was even more resentful of the Old Arbitrator's call of ball two on his second pitch. When Klem called the next pitch a ball too, the kid pitcher couldn't take it any longer. He stormed in off the mound and raged at the wispy-haired old umpire, the granddaddy of his profession. "It was right on the corner!" he argued. "Anybody could see it was a strike!"

"It looked like a ball to me," Klem said mildly, waving the pitcher back to the mound. But when the next pitch came in, and Musial uncoiled that magnificent swing of his and lined a double cleanly into right-center field, Klem couldn't resist walking out toward the unhappy pitcher. "Son," he said softly, "when it's a strike, Mr. Musial will let you know."

I've always enjoyed good umpire stories, mostly, I guess, because I've always admired good umpires. I've drawn a lot of laughs at winter banquet tables telling about old Steamboat Johnson, one of the first of baseball's colorful umpires. Steamboat was never bashful about making his calls behind the plate, and he picked up his share of enemies. One day, umpiring in Memphis in the old Southern Association, he found himself under constant attack by a lady rooter for the home team. She kept after him all afternoon; every time he called a ball, she insisted it was a strike; every time he called a runner safe, she insisted he should have been out. Finally, when he waved a Memphis man out at the plate on a close play, the lady stood up in the grandstand and screamed, "Johnson, if I was your wife, I'd put poison in your coffee!" Steamboat ripped off his mask and stepped a few paces away from the plate, faced the stands, and hollered back, "Lady, if I was your husband, I'd take it!"

Then there was the anonymous, and perhaps apocryphal, umpire who had to deal with the temperamental ballplayer who liked to throw his bat in the air by way of criticizing a decision. One day the chronic complainer, objecting to a called third strike, heaved his bat angrily over his head. The ump, watching the Louisville Slugger sail into the air, said calmly, "Son, if that bat comes down, you're out of the ball game!"

I don't mean to put too much emphasis on the jokes about umpiring. To me it's one of the most important aspects of the game. Bill Klem said it better than anybody else when he told a writer many years ago: "I never thought eyesight was the most important thing in umpiring. The most important things are guts, honesty, common sense, a desire for fair play and an understanding of human nature."

There is a story about Larry Goetz, one of the greatest of the modern National League—or any league—umpires, having lunch one day with Warren Giles, the president of his league, and Waite Hoyt. When the captain put the menus on the table, Goetz reached into his breast pocket and took out a pair of eyeglasses. "Larry," Hoyt kidded him, "you've got a lot of nerve, an umpire, putting

on glasses in front of the league president." "I have to have a lot of
nerve," Goetz said, "or I wouldn't be an umpire."

All of us who were in Yankee Stadium on Monday, September 26,
1949, when the Yankees lost a 7–6 ball game to the Boston Red Sox
with the American League pennant hanging in the balance in one
of the closest races on record, will always remember the courage of
umpire Bill Grieve. The Red Sox scored four runs in the eighth
inning to win the game, and the last of those four runs was carried
in by Johnny Pesky—who became the manager of the Sox in
1963, fourteen years later. Pesky was bunted home by Bobby Doerr.
Doerr's bunt went to Tommy Henrich, who was playing first base
for the Yankees; Henrich fielded the ball cleanly and threw it as
straight as a clothesline to catcher Ralph Houk—who, in 1961, became the manager of the Yankees. Bill Grieve, sixteen years a professional umpire and twelve years in the American League, was behind the plate, and he called Pesky safe. The Yankees swarmed all
over him as the 65,156 spectators went wild.

Houk grabbed Grieve and shoved him as hard as he could. Manager Casey Stengel charged out of the Yankees' dugout and laid
hands violently on the umpire. Half the ball club stormed and raged
around the plate. But it didn't do any good; Pesky was safe, and
safe he remained. Not even the unfortunate, blindly angry question
of Yankee outfielder Cliff Mapes made any difference. "How much
did you have on the game?" Mapes yelled at Grieve, for which he
paid a fine of $200 to the American League office. (Houk and Sten-
gel got away with $150 each.) It didn't make any difference that
the matchless Yankee relief pitcher, Joe Page, showed his displeasure
by throwing his glove as high into the air as he could. Pesky was
still safe.

"Under the rules," Red Smith wrote the next day in his newspaper column, "Mr. Grieve was clearly entitled to lift the im-
perious thumb not once but thrice. However, he knows Houk for
a hustling, combative operative who was unmistakably sincere in

his conviction that the umpire had booted the play. . . . Willie kept his temper. In their moment of greatest need, he declined to deprive the Yankees of the services of their manager, their relief pitcher, and the only able-bodied catcher then available. He should have been saluted for it, not vilified."

That, I suppose, is too much to ask of a ball club that has just lost a vitally important end-of-season game on a close decision by an umpire. But it shouldn't be. Umpires rarely pay any attention to charges of incompetence leveled at them under such circumstances because they know that good judgment has been washed away by anger and disappointment. They know that a decision as close and as crucial as the Pesky decision is bound to be hailed as "a great call" by one side and "the worst umpiring I ever saw" by the other side. But, in my opinion, the rules and traditions of the game should make it unthinkable for any player or manager to shout personal accusations at an umpire. The record of the profession over all these years deserves better treatment.

There's one other point, too, and Red Smith made it the same day he wrote about Bill Grieve and Cliff Mapes and Ralph Houk and Casey Stengel and Joe Page. "In the excitement," Red said, "one point has been generally overlooked. That is that the Yankees did not lose because of an umpire's decision. They lost because they played bad baseball and booted away a three-run lead."

Anybody, of course, can lose his head in a moment of overpowering excitement, but I have noticed over the years that the best ballplayers give the umpires the least trouble. Not one of the truly great players of our time has been known as an umpire-fighter. Call the roll: Stan Musial, Ted Williams, Joe DiMaggio, Mickey Mantle, Bob Feller, Willie Mays, Warren Spahn, Whitey Ford—they played the game and let the umpires call them. Two topflight players who did tangle with the umpires fairly often were Yogi Berra and Jackie Robinson, but even these firebrands kept their protests within rea-

sonable bounds and, like Frank Frisch of an earlier era, tried to
leave their complaints on the ball field and not allow them to inter-
fere with their friendly relationships with the umpires as men.

It seems to me there is a lot of good sense in something Frank
Dascoli, one of the best of the modern National League umpires,
once said: "The job of the umpire has been made tougher by the
increasing lack of respect for authority that exists in the United
States today. When I was a kid things were different. If you had
some trouble with your teacher in school, for instance, your parents
backed up the teacher and made you get into line—or else. Now,
more often than not, they back up the kid and go to the school and
complain to the principal that the teacher is being unfair. Police-
men don't get the respect they ought to get. Even the government
doesn't. So when people who are conditioned by this kind of an attitude come out to the ball park, they aren't going to respect the
umpire—and that goes for ballplayers and fans alike."

It is, of course, too much to ask that people should stop making
jokes about umpires. Umpire jokes have been with us as long as the
game of baseball and will be with us as long as the game endures.
One of the oldest, brought up to date every now and then to suit
some newcomer to the ranks of controversial umpires, goes like this.
I'll take the name of the great Bill Klem in vain only because his
name is the symbol of the umpire for all of us. "Klem had called
a few close ones against the Giants in this particular series, and
the Giants were steaming at him. Then, a few days later, he showed
up at the pass gate with a couple of friends and asked to have them
admitted along with him. 'I can't do it,' the man at the turnstile
protested. 'Mr. Stoneham has issued written orders that nobody
is to be admitted without a regular pass.' He thought it over. 'I'll
tell you what I'll do,' he said finally. 'I'll send up a note to
Mr. Stoneham's office and ask him to send down a couple of passes.'
A few minutes went by and then a note came down from the office.

The guard looked at it and passed it over to Klem. 'Let them in,' it read. 'If there are two men in New York brave enough to say they are friends of Bill Klem, pass them in and give them box seats.' "

Then there is the standard joke about the base runner making a desperate slide into second base trying to beat a force play. The runner might be Elston Howard, not noted for his speed afoot, and the umpire might be Jim Honochick. "I made it! I made it!" Ellie begins to yell as soon as he slides into the bag. Honochick, his thumb majestically hoisted into the air, looks down at him interestedly and says gently, "You sure did, Ellie. But what detained you?"

One of the better versions of the many jokes about umpires putting angry managers out of the game is this one, supposed to have originated with Frank Frisch. The old Fordham Flash was having his ups and downs with one of his favorite antagonists, George Magerkurth, and had already gone a few rounds with him when Magerkurth infuriated him with another call that Frank regarded as a bad one. The manager of the St. Louis Gas House Gang roared out of his dugout and stormed up to the plate. Then, ham that he always was in his assaults upon the men in blue, Frank stopped short, held out his arms as if imploring heaven, and fell flat on his face on the ground. It was, he was telling the crowd dramatically, more than any mortal could be expected to bear. Magerkurth, understandably, was not amused. He stalked over to the fallen manager, prodded him rudely with his foot, and said grimly, "Frisch, dead or alive, you're out of the ball game!"

Then there is the psychic ejection. The manager rushes out to protest a decision, and before he can open his mouth, the umpire has waved him out of the ball park. "But I didn't even say a word!" the dumbfounded manager screams. "Get out of here," says the umpire. "I know what you're thinking!"

Jimmy Dykes, for many years one of the busiest and most traveled managers in the American League, is generally credited with the George Moriarty joke. Moriarty was a good umpire and a stalwart citizen; he could take care of himself in any kind of argument on the ball field. But Dykes deflated him the day he walked up to him after a big hassle over a called third strike and said, in a deceptively mild way, "I beg your pardon, Mr. Moriarty, but would you mind telling me how you spell your last name?" The umpire was surprised, but he obliged Jimmy. He spelled out his name carefully, letter by letter. Dykes nodded thoughtfully. "Just as I thought," he said. "Only one 'i.' "

Another Dykes story that I believe to be true concerns a day Jimmy was managing the Chicago White Sox in a game at Fenway Park. The Red Sox put on a big rally in the late stages of the game and Jimmy's early lead disappeared fast. He used up pitchers so quickly that he didn't have anybody warmed up when he wanted to make another change, so he tried every way he knew of stalling and finally tried calling for a bullpen tenant who hadn't warmed up at all. When this gentleman had slowly walked the long walk in from the bullpen, while the pitcher Dykes really wanted was still throwing frantically, Jimmy rushed out to the umpire. "I'm terribly sorry," he apologized, "but we got our wires crossed. This isn't the guy we want. I'll get my man right away." "Oh, no, you won't," the umpire growled. "This guy is here and this guy pitches. Let's go." Dykes argued ferociously but it didn't do him any good. The "cold" pitcher had to pitch after a handful of warm-up throws, and the Red Sox fell on him like a hungry lion falling on a lamb. The White Sox lost the game. The next day Mule Haas, one of Dykes' coaches, took the lineup out to home plate before the game. There were eight names on it, no pitcher. When the plate umpire raised his eyebrows, Mule pointed to yesterday's offender, now stationed at first base in the way of the usual umpires' rotation. "My boss says *he'll* pick the pitcher," Mule said, "just like he did yesterday."

Maybe the best umpire story, though, is another Bill Klem anecdote that isn't a joke at all. It strikes to the heart of the matter.

They say that one day John McGraw, the angriest of all managers, stormed Klem and, standing head to head and toe to toe with him, let Klem know that he had taken all he was going to take from a lousy umpire and that he was going to do something about it. "I'm going all the way to the top, Klem," he raged, "and I'm going to get your job, so help me." Klem stood his ground calmly. "Mr. McGraw," he said, "if it's possible for you to get my job, I don't want it."

Another little story that sometimes is told as a joke seems to me to be more serious than funny and more than a little revealing about the art of umpiring and the dedication of the men who umpire. Many years ago, I am told, when Ban Johnson was the president of the American League, he had on his staff an umpire named Dick Nallin. One day Nallin was involved in a protested ball game. The protesting manager swore that the umpire had insisted on making the decision on a key play that had taken place behind his back. Nallin didn't deny it, so Johnson sent him a telegram asking for an explanation of how, if the play had indeed been behind his back, he had arrived at his decision. Undisturbed, Nallin fired back his answer: "The animal instinct of an umpire."

If it's possible to top that one at all, which I doubt, it would have to be with the old story Joe McCarthy used to tell about the time he dreamed he had died and gone to heaven. St. Peter told him that they had been waiting for him for a long time and that they wanted him to pick the best All-Star team he could find in heaven and get ready to manage it in a do-or-die series with the All-Stars from the other place. Joe agreed with pleasure, and it didn't take him long to assemble a tremendous team from such ballplayers as Lou Gehrig, Walter Johnson, Wee Willie Keeler, Eddie Collins, Honus Wagner, Ty Cobb, Tris Speaker and Babe Ruth. "Nobody could ever beat this team," Joe reported to St. Peter. "You can challenge the Devil any time you want." It surprised St. Peter, then, that the Devil accepted the challenge cheerfully; he didn't seem the least bit worried. "You really haven't got a chance of winning," St. Peter said charitably. "We've got every good ballplayer who ever lived." "I know," said the Devil, "but I've got all the umpires."

No umpire could possibly call every play right—not in a single ball game much less in a whole season. It would require a complicated and expensive electronic system to flash an infallible answer on one play alone—the race between runner and ball to first base. Inevitably, every season will produce fusses such as the memorable one that occurred in the World Series of 1952 when umpire Art Passarella called Johnny Sain of the Yankees out on a close play at first base and the next day's newspapers printed a picture showing Sain's foot firmly planted on the bag as first baseman Gil Hodges of the Dodgers reached out toward Jackie Robinson's throw, still hanging big and white in the air, two or three feet short of the bag.

"It looks like Passarella called a wrong play," Commissioner Ford Frick said when he was asked to comment on the picture. "But if he did, he's only human. I assure you it's not the first wrong call ever made by an umpire, if it was that. What's all the shouting about? Players make mistakes, too."

Charlie Dressen, the manager of the Dodgers, smarting under the barrage of Yankee criticism of the play, said defensively, "Are you sure that's the ball? How do you know somebody didn't paint that ball into the picture?" That got Casey Stengel's goat. "Tell him," Casey said hotly, "it sure as hell ain't a sea gull."

All of which brings you back to what Bill Klem meant when he said, over and over again, "I never missed one yet." I once asked him if he really meant that he had never made a mistake on a call in his life. "That's not what I'm getting at at all," he said. "I may have missed one or two a game, maybe one or two hundred a season. But I never missed one in my heart."

Chapter 6

Catching a ball is a pleasure; knowing what
to do with it after you catch it is a
business.—TOMMY HENRICH

I never met anybody, in or out of baseball, who didn't
like Tommy Henrich.

There's a lot to like about him. The way he played ball—so surely,
so skillfully and so professionally that my nickname for him, "Old
Reliable," stuck throughout his baseball career because it so plainly
suited him. His unfailing courtesy. His integrity, his quiet but deep
respect for himself both as a ballplayer and as a man, and his
willingness to respect you for what you were. His inquiring, vigorous
mind, with its astonishingly wide range of interests. His love of
music. His genuine, warm interest in people. His sense of humor.

It was a treat to listen to this amiable, articulate man sit around
with a few friends after a ball game and tell stories. Like the one
about the old-timer who couldn't hit lefties to save his life. He was
out of the game for a few years during World War II, and naturally
when he got back into the lineup for the first time after the war
the other club put in a lefty to pitch. "You should have seen this
guy," Tom said. "He was so mad he was shaking. He actually waved

his fist at the poor pitcher, who didn't know him from Adam. 'A hundred thousand of you left-handed bums they sent overseas in this war,' he yelled out to the pitcher's box, 'and I'll bet every damn one of you came back.' "

More than most major-leaguers, Tommy had a great knack for distinguishing between baseball for fun and baseball for business. One of his more famous lines, repeated many times by admiring reporters, was, "Catching a ball is a pleasure; knowing what to do with it after you catch it is a business." Once he said, "I like to play baseball at a picnic—you know, the married men against the single men or something like that. But when you're out there against clubs like Boston and Cleveland, it's not all fun. Especially when you go for the horse-collar."

I don't know anybody except Tommy Henrich who could have gone so calmly and so successfully through a day like the one he had in the late summer of 1942, the first year of the war. He took his wife Eileen to the hospital in the morning, and before noon she had presented their first child to him, a boy, Thomas David, forever after to be known simply as T.D. As soon as he knew his wife and son were all right, Tommy took off for the Stadium and a double-header with Washington. He broke up the first game with a home run. Joe McCarthy let him sit out the second game until he needed a pinch hitter in the seventh inning, and then Tommy went up to bat and hit another home run. When the game was over he took a shower, got dressed quickly, caught a train to Cleveland and enlisted in the Coast Guard. And that's Tommy Henrich for you.

"Strictly Massillon, Ohio," somebody once wrote about Tommy, kidding him about his midwestern fondness for home and family, a thick ham sandwich and a cold beer, and homey amusements like barbershop-quartet singing. Well, he does come from Massillon— lives there again now, as a matter of fact—and no matter how many years he was away, living and visiting in the biggest cities in the country, he never lost his old habits or convictions or principles.

But there never was anything small-town or backwoods about
Tommy's approach to baseball. He always studied the game as
though he were about to take a final examination in it. He worried
about the shadows in the outfield, the force of the wind and its
effect on a fly ball, the hardness or softness of the turf and the
difference it might make in the hop of a ground ball, and about
what he knew of the past-performance chart of this particular hitter against this particular pitcher. He wasn't the only outfielder
in the big leagues who took his job seriously; he just seemed to take
it a little more seriously, and work at it a little harder, than almost
anybody else.

Tommy had higher batting averages in other years—he hit .320
in 67 games in 1937, the year he broke in—but I think the most
typically Henrich of all his many years with the Yankees was 1949,
the year the team won its first pennant for Casey Stengel. He hit
.287 that year, a solid, respectable figure, especially for a ballplayer
pretty well along in years, but his average didn't even begin to re-
flect what he meant to the ball club or how much he had to do
with the winning of the pennant and the World Series. The Yankees and their fans were depressed by Joe DiMaggio's heel troubles
at the beginning of the season; they doubted their chances of making it with the big fellow out of the lineup. So on Opening Day at
the Stadium, April 19, Henrich hit a two-run homer in the last
of the ninth to turn a looming 2–1 defeat into a 3–2 victory. And
from then on, all through the long 65-game stretch when DiMaggio couldn't play and just wandered restlessly from hospital room
to hotel room, chain-smoking cigarettes and growing more irritable
and more pessimistic day by day, it was Tommy Henrich who
picked up the ball club and carried it on his back until he had convinced everybody that the Yankees not only could win but would
win. It was Henrich who hit the big home runs in the pinch, made
the spectacular catches, kept the rallies alive, and provided the reliable power source that every pennant-caliber ball club must gen-

erate somewhere in the batting order. It wasn't all just hitting and fielding and base running, either; it was the inspiration and the confidence that came from having a man like him on your side.

There was plenty of solid accomplishment, too. At the end of those first 65 games the Yankees held first place by 4½ games, and Henrich personally had provided the winning margin in exactly 18 games. He had hit 16 home runs in that stretch, and 12 of them had been the crucial hit of the game. Milton Gross of the New York *Post* put together a log of Tommy's game-saving contributions, and it looked like this:

April 19, he beat the Senators with a ninth-inning, two-out homer.

April 20, his fourth-inning home run scored the first run in a 1–0 win over Washington.

April 21, his hit put Johnny Lindell into scoring position as Yanks defeated Senators, 2–1.

April 22, he was on base four out of five times as Yanks defeated Red Sox, 5–3.

April 30, his two-run, two-out, ninth-inning homer beat the Red Sox, 4–3.

May 3, his double drove in the winning run in the eighth inning as Yanks defeated St. Louis Browns, 5–3.

May 10, his triple brought in the first two runs as Yanks defeated Tigers, 6–1.

May 16, his seventh-inning homer defeated Cleveland, 4–3.

May 17, his two home runs defeated Bob Feller and the Indians, 6–0.

May 23, his first-inning, three-run homer got Yanks started on a 10–3 win over the Browns.

May 27, his first-inning home run beat the Athletics, 3–0.

June 1, his seventh-inning homer broke a scoreless tie and put the Yankees on the road to a 3–0 win over the White Sox.

June 2, his three-run, first-inning homer started a 12–7 rout of the White Sox.

June 14, his home run and double drove in five runs as the Yankees defeated the White Sox, 15–3.

June 22, his sixth-inning homer contributed two runs to defeat of the Browns, 10–8.

June 23, he started off 12–0 win over Tigers with a three-run home run in the first inning, batted in five runs altogether.

June 24, his single in the seventh inning broke a 4–4 tie and defeated the Tigers, 5–4.

June 26, his two-run single in the eighth inning broke a 2–2 tie and started the Yanks on a 6–2 win over the Tigers in the first game of a doubleheader.

June 26, Tigers got off winging with two runs in the first inning of the second half of the doubleheader, Henrich tied it up with a two-run home run, but the Tigers pulled away again to win easily.

As Gross said, what did you expect Henrich to do, win them all by himself?

In those days *Sport* magazine gave a big awards dinner at the end of the year. They would bring together hundreds of the biggest names in sports for the affair, at the Hotel Astor in New York and present a trophy to the top performer of the year in each major sport. The *pièce de résistance* was the presentation of a special award to the Athlete of the Year, the champion of champions, the man who best combined the attributes of skill, courage, inspiration and character. The award had gone to Joe DiMaggio in 1947 and to Lou Boudreau, the player-manager of the world champion Cleveland Indians, in 1948. In 1949 it was Tommy's, and no one ever deserved it more. A whole platoon of baseball celebrities applauded him when he stepped up to accept the award—Jackie Robinson, Yogi Berra, Allie Reynolds, Joe Page, Gene Woodling, Don Newcombe, Gil Hodges, Roy Campanella, Bob Feller, Bobby Thomson, Lou Boudreau, Hank Greenberg, Frank Frisch, and even Tyrus Raymond Cobb, the old Georgia Peach. Then Branch Rickey took over the microphone and delivered one of his patented speeches, eloquent, provocative, authoritative and literate. When he finished, Tommy leaned over to the man sitting next to him on the dais and said admiringly, but with that devastating Henrich honesty, "It was a hell of a speech. I'll bet there isn't a man in the hall who understood a word of it."

Tommy played for the Yankees for so many years, and played so vital a part in so many Yankee pennants, that it's hard to remember that he wasn't always a Yankee. But he wasn't. As a good Ohioan, he grew up rooting fervently for the Cleveland Indians, and it was the ambition of his life to play for Cleveland. He hoped that he was well on his way toward his goal when the Indians signed him to a contract with their Zanesville, Ohio, farm team, in 1934. Tommy was eighteen that year. Two years later, in 1936, he hit .346 for the New Orleans club of the Southern Association, and felt, when he went home at the end of the season, that he was on his way to the Indians at last. But he heard nothing about being promoted to the big team. All he did hear, and all he read about, were rumors that he was to be traded—here, there or somewhere else. To the Boston Braves (they were called the Bees then) or to the St. Louis Browns. Finally, the Indians told him he was supposed to report for 1937 spring training with the Milwaukee Brewers, still another Cleveland farm operation.

That made Henrich mad. He didn't see why his record didn't entitle him at least to a trial with the Indians. So he sat down and wrote a polite but bold letter to Commissioner Kenesaw Mountain Landis, not a bit backward about making the charge that the Cleveland club was illegally trying to "cover him up" and thus prevent his advancement into the major leagues until such time as they were good and ready to use him themselves. While he was waiting for an answer from the Judge, Tommy engaged in a brisk correspondence with Lou Nahim, the business manager of the Brewers. Nahim had offered Henrich a contract that Tommy thought fell far short of reflecting the good season he had had at New Orleans. He protested, and Nahim upped his price a little, defending his position by saying that American Association rules limited each club to a salary ceiling of $8,000 per month for twenty players—necessitating, he pointed out, an average salary of approximately $400 per month per man. Tommy was unimpressed and said so. "I compliment you on signing your players at the lowest possible figures," he wrote. "I realize it is sound business. I understand your attitude toward average salary. But, Mr. Nahim, I am not an average ballplayer and never intend to be one."

Nahim wrote back asking Tommy to put himself in the position of a club owner trying to find a way to sign twenty players under the $8,000 monthly limit, and suggesting that with five .300 hitters and a few first-class pitchers on the club, all looking for high salaries, Tommy wouldn't find it so easy either. Undaunted, our man Henrich wrote back: "Your letter impressed me a good deal. I appreciate your frank discussion. I am not prepared as yet to give my plan as owner. I think the matter needs a few more days consideration. It must, because you've had all winter to think it over and haven't hit on the right solution yet. . . . Nevertheless, I'll offer you my ideas on the subject within a short time. You'll have to overlook some of the flaws because of my inexperience in the business side of baseball and because I am just a rookie ballplayer. However, if you're impressed by it, well, I wouldn't object to a position in the executive department, where I understand the real money is made."

When he finally agreed on a wage, Tommy told Nahim, characteristically, "Will report in good shape, ready to give you my best."

Fortunately for Henrich, and unfortunately for Nahim and the Milwaukee club, Tommy spent only a few days with the Brewers in spring training. Judge Landis held two hearings on his case and decided that the Indians had indeed violated baseball law by putting him out on option more than three times, just as Tommy had claimed. They had turned down offers for his contract made by both the Red Sox, for $30,000, and the Giants, for $40,000, and had tried to keep him on ice until they had a spot for him on their own roster. The Judge declared Tommy a free agent—and the offers poured in from all sides. The ball clubs weren't throwing around bonus checks quite so freely in those days as they do now, but they were all willing to back up with cash their conviction that Henrich had the look of a big-league hitter. Tommy considered each offer carefully and finally decided that he would take the Yankees' offer of a $25,000 bonus. His first contract with the club called for only $6,000, but in his second season he got a good raise and also picked up the first of a string of World Series checks, this one for $5,836.

By 1949 the Yankees were paying Tommy $40,000 per season, and were glad to do it. I've always remembered something Casey Stengel said about him that year. "Henrich," Casey said, "is the kind of man every manager wants to have playing for him. You can manage practically all your life and never come across a fellow like him. I'm lucky. I've got him now. You don't have to lay down any rules for him or give him any orders. He knows what's best for himself and for the team, and he goes ahead and does it."

It's too bad that Tommy's career couldn't have gone on longer. He had a great deal of trouble with his left knee, which he first injured during those few days he trained with the Brewers in 1937, before he signed with the Yankees and went up to New York. ("I'll never forget the bellboy who showed me to my hotel room," Tommy told me once. "He really gave me a hard time. 'So you're Henrich,' he said. 'The papers say you're going to break into the lineup right away. Hey, wait till you see DiMaggio and Hoag and Selkirk. You ever seen those guys play?' I wasn't going to let him walk all over me, so I said, right back at him, 'You ever see Henrich play?' ") The knee bothered him off and on all through his career with the Yankees, and finally forced him to retire at the end of the 1950 season.

The bad knee did one good thing for Tommy. It got him a wonderful wife. He tore some ligaments in the knee on the last day of August in 1940 and had to spend a month in St. Elizabeth's Hospital in New York. One of his nurses was a pretty Irish girl, Eileen

O'Reilly, who knew nothing about baseball and had never heard of Tommy Henrich but who became curious about him when the doctors kept coming around to meet "the celebrity." "He looked just like any other patient to me when I first saw him," Eileen said, "except that maybe there was more food and fruit in his room. Oh, yes, and he always had his radio turned on to classical music. Frankly, I was more intrigued with the food and the fruit and the music than I was with the patient."

Tommy always laughs at Eileen when she teases him like that. "I took her to Lewisohn Stadium, to one of those outdoor concerts, on our first date," he said. "That's how I got her. She was so surprised that a ballplayer could enjoy a concert that she married me."

Even though she was married to an important baseball player all those years, Eileen Henrich never has interested herself particularly in baseball. "Frankly," she said once, "there were plenty of days when I didn't have any idea at all what happened at the ball park. With the kids and the house to worry about, there always was enough else to talk about when Tommy came home. Maybe I've taken Tommy's ability for granted all these years, but if people didn't insist on talking to me about my husband I really wouldn't know if he were a good or bad ballplayer. I do know this, though. He's a good husband and father."

Tommy has his own favorite domestic story. "There once was an old-time ballplayer, and a terrific hitter," he said, "named Jay Kirke. His wife used to follow the games religiously, and every afternoon when he came home from the ball park she'd sing this little ditty to him:

> *Well, my honey, well, my Jay,*
> *How many hits did you get today?*

"That was all right when old Jay was getting his hits," Tommy says, "but when he wasn't, it wasn't. Finally, one afternoon, he waited until she got all through with the silly little ditty and he

No matter how much attention is paid to the men who are actually playing the game, the noncombatants hold their share of the stage too. Like Leo Durocher, showing a Dodger ballplayer how to bunt; Al Lopez, mulling over a change in White Sox pitchers; Ralph Houk, telling the press about his move from the Yankee dugout to the front office; or a career manager like Lou Boudreau, sitting in the dugout wishing there were some way he could help the kids do it the way he used to do it.

Here are a couple of victory pictures that will be hanging at Yankee Stadium for a long time. That's Don Larsen throwing the last pitch of his historic perfect game against the Dodgers in the World Series of 1956, and Hank Bauer carrying the winning run across

the plate to beat the Dodgers in the last game of the '53 series. It looks as though Frankie Crosetti is chasing Hank across the plate, taking no chances.

Above, the greatest of all the modern Yankees, a fit companion for Babe Ruth and Lou Gehrig, is Joseph Paul DiMaggio, who hit safely in 56 games in a row in the season of 1941 and who still shows up at spring camp every March to help such players as Yogi Berra *(left)* and Ralph Houk teach the young Yankees how to master the art of hitting the baseball.

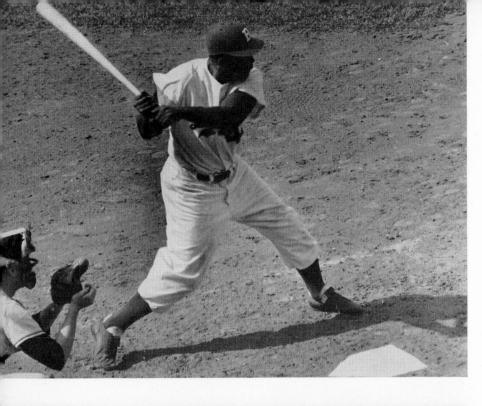

There were some superlative ballplayers on view in the majors in the years after World War II. Like pigeon-toed Jackie Robinson of the Brooklyn Dodgers, free-swinging Willie Mays of the New York (and San Francisco) Giants, the inimitable Stan Musial of the St. Louis Cardinals, glowering Early Wynn of the Cleveland Indians and the Chicago White Sox, and impetuous Ted Williams of the Boston Red Sox—perhaps the greatest hitter of his time.

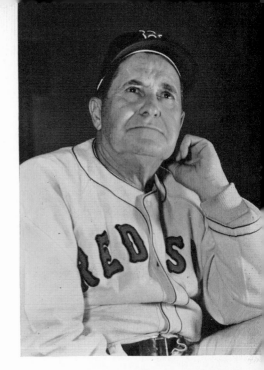

One of the reasons why the Yankees win so many pennants is the tradition that stands behind them. Young Yankees think of Babe Ruth running across the plate after hitting his 60th home run in 1927, and Lou Gehrig holding out his hand to congratulate him; they think of Ruth and Gehrig shaking hands with Paul and Lloyd Waner of the Pirates and then demolishing them in the World Series of 1927; they think of Joe McCarthy, who helped set the Yankee pattern before he moved on to manage the Red Sox; and they think of old number 3 saying goodbye to the crowd on Babe Ruth Day in 1947. They remember, and they try to live up to it.

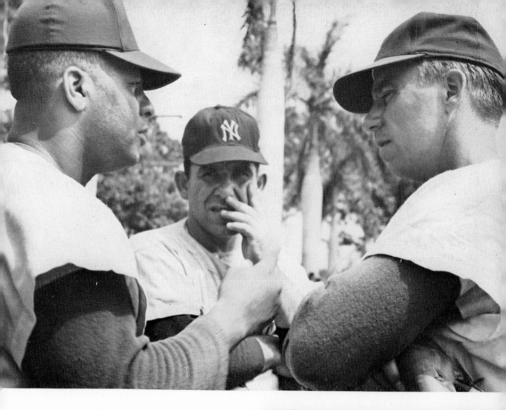

There is only one Yogi Berra. Whether he is making an unintentionally funny speech to the fans on his special "day," swinging the bat in that wonderfully effortless way that produced more home runs than any other big-league catcher ever hit, listening carefully to rival ballplayers like Roy Campanella and Peewee Reese, or giving signals from a seat in the corner of the dugout, Yogi can always hold his own.

Baseball has known fewer more destructive one-two batting punches than the M&M combination of the Yankees, Mickey Mantle *(left)* and Roger Maris. In 1961 they hit 115 home runs between them, 61 for Maris and 54 for Mantle. Each could swing with pulverizing power; Maris could make amazing catches, too, and Mantle could run the bases like a frightened deer. Together, they could do it all.

Being the Yankees' play-by-play announcer brings you into contact with people in all walks of life. I met the late President John F. Kennedy at the Waldorf, Ted Williams at St. Petersburg, Florida, a yard full of inmates at Indiana State Prison, a bunch of kids outside Yankee Stadium and a bunch of adults outside Freehold Raceway, and officers and men of the U.S. Navy at our big base on Guantanamo Bay in Cuba.

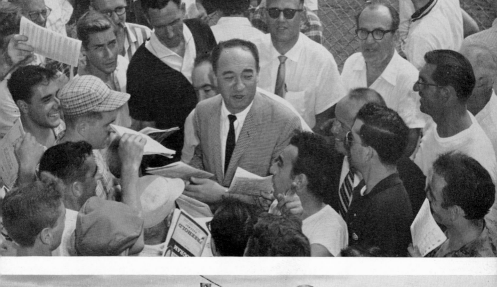

No man of his time—and he goes back a very long way—has done more than Casey Stengel to make baseball the national game. Bringing a relief pitcher into the game, exhorting his ball club from the dugout, giving the word to the reporters whose job he made so much easier, running out his home run in the 1923 World Series or posing for a picture with rival World Series manager Walter Alston, Casey was always Casey.

And sometimes Casey could look like a painting by Rembrandt.

hollered at her, 'Look, you take care of the cooking in this family and I'll take care of the hitting!' " Tommy always takes a long pull on his cigar at this point, then winks and says, with satisfaction, "My wife takes care of the cooking."

A great man, Tommy Henrich, and a great Yankee. The New York chapter of the Baseball Writers Association threw a dinner for Tommy, Charlie Keller and Joe DiMaggio in January of 1950 and told the boys that they constituted one of the great outfields of baseball history. That's the truth. And it's also the truth that a ball club which has boasted Babe Ruth and Joe DiMaggio and Yogi Berra and Mickey Mantle has known very few stars the equal of modest, industrious, always honorable Tommy Henrich. If Tommy were reading over my shoulder right now, he would probably nudge me and say, "Don't forget to tell them I was a pretty good ballplayer, too." He was.

Chapter 7

The Declaration of Independence says all
men are created equal—not all men except
Negroes.—ADLAI E. STEVENSON

IF, in the middle of the 1963 baseball season, you were
trying to put together the best all-star team you could think of,
drawing from the finest talent in both major leagues, you might
have done a lot worse than to come up with Bill White of the St.
Louis Cardinals at first base, Julian Javier of the Cardinals at second
base, Jim Gilliam of the Los Angeles Dodgers at third base, and
Maury Wills of the Dodgers at shortstop; Leon Wagner of the Los
Angeles Angels in left field, Willie Mays of the San Francisco Giants
in center field, and Hank Aaron of the Milwaukee Braves in right
field; Elston Howard of the New York Yankees as the catcher, and
Juan Pizarro of the Chicago White Sox as the pitcher. It would be
quite a ball club, and in addition to its impressive batting, fielding
and pitching records it would have one other extraordinary qualification—every one of those nine men is a Negro.

When you consider that the first Negro to play in the major
leagues was Jackie Robinson of the Brooklyn Dodgers, in 1947, it is
hard to realize that in just over fifteen years so many colored men

have achieved so much success in the game. Most historians of the Negro's fight for equal opportunity in America consider the breaking of the color line in baseball to be a historic turning point in the struggle. Long before the sit-in strikes, the mass demonstrations, the boycotts and the other manifestations of the uprising, a handful of Negroes in major-league baseball—first Jackie Robinson, then Larry Doby and Roy Campanella and Don Newcombe and Henry Thompson and others—were establishing the first meaningful postwar beachhead of the black man in the white man's America.

It wasn't easy to get all the mayors and sheriffs of the sun-flooded Florida communities where most big-league ball clubs do their spring training to accept the coming of the Negro. Many of these communities had ordinances prohibiting integrated competition. In Sanford, Florida, in 1946, Jackie Robinson was ordered off the field by a red-necked sheriff who wasn't about to have "any nigger ballplayer" on a white man's baseball field. Jackie, who was with the Montreal Royals then, had made it through batting practice and infield practice, and had lined a single to center field when he came up second in the Royals' batting order. He had even managed to steal second and slide home safely on a single by Tom Tatum. But that was as far as he was allowed to go. To steal a phrase from the title of a recent Peter Sellers movie, the wrong arm of the law got him out of there before he could do any more damage to the sanctity of the ball park.

When the season ended, though, with the Royals beating the Louisville Colonels in the Louisville ball park in the last game of the International League's championship play-off round, Jackie hit a triple, double and single and practically won the game for Montreal all by himself. You might think the 20,000 Southerners in the stands would have resented him bitterly. But instead they cheered him generously even as he beat their own ball club into the ground. And when the game was over and the Royals were celebrating in the visitors' clubhouse, an usher came in to ask Robinson if he

would step outside and wave to the crowd of thousands clamoring
for him. If he didn't, they might never go home. When he finally
was able to get dressed and leave, Jackie had to run for his car
through a sea of applauding, autograph-seeking fans. "It was," said
Sam Maltin, a Louisville sportswriter, "probably the only day in
the history of the South that a black man ran from a white mob
with love instead of lynching on its mind."

Those early days of Robinson's trail-blazing seem long ago and
far away when you think of the number of fine Negro baseball
players in the major leagues today. When Jackie was a rookie, there
were many clubs who had no thought of signing Negro ballplayers;
today, with twenty clubs in the two leagues, there is not one all-
white team. In a typical big series in the National League, in the
summer of 1963, with the Giants playing their California rivals, the
Dodgers, you would have seen men like Willie Mays, Orlando Ce-
peda and Willie McCovey flexing their muscles against men like
Maury Wills, Tommy and Willie Davis, Jim Gilliam and John Rose-
boro—Negroes all. If you paid your way in to watch the Yankees
play the Minnesota Twins you would see Elston Howard, Hector
Lopez and maybe relief pitcher Marshall Bridges in the uniform of
the Yankees and Zoilo Versalles, Vic Power, Earl Battey and Camilo
Pascual performing for the Twins. When Jackie Robinson won the
Sporting News award as the rookie of the year in the National
League for 1947, the newspaper felt obliged to point out: "In select-
ing the outstanding rookie of 1947, the *Sporting News* sifted and
weighed only stark baseball values. That Jack Roosevelt Robinson
might have had more obstacles than his first-year competitors, and
that he perhaps had a harder fight to gain even major-league recognition, is no concern of this publication. The sociological experiment that Robinson represented, the trail-blazing that he did, the
barriers he broke down, did not enter into the decision. He was
rated and examined solely as a freshman player in the big leagues
—on the basis of his hitting, his running, his defensive play, his

team value." Today, when one of baseball's important awards is
won by a Negro, nobody bothers to explain that it was given him
only on the basis of his performance on the field. We have come a
long way.

More and more major-league ball clubs are changing their traditional billeting arrangements for spring training in order to provide
accommodations for all of their players, white and colored. The
clubs training in Arizona and California, the Giants, Red Sox, Indians, Cubs, Angels and Colts, have no problem. But things are
changing rapidly in Florida, too. All the Yankees live together comfortably at the Yankee Clipper Motel in Fort Lauderdale. The
Dodgers own their own layout at Vero Beach, a former naval training base which they bought from the United States government,
and they do exactly as they please there. The Cincinnati Reds
acquired ownership of the Tampa Terrace Hotel in Tampa and
don't have to worry about where they will find living quarters for
Frank Robinson, Vada Pinson and their other Negro stars. The
Cardinals used to have to find separate hotel living quarters for
their unmarried Negro players, but now all the bachelor ballplayers
live in the same hotel. The Phillies left their long-time spring training headquarters in Clearwater because their Negro players weren't
allowed to bunk there, but after a season or two the club was asked
to come back—intact. That's progress. Year after year you see in
the newspapers little items such as this one that appeared in March
of 1961 under the headline "Braves Remove Segregation Barrier at
Bradenton Park" and that went on to say: "The Milwaukee Braves
have announced an end to racial segregation at exhibition games at
their spring training base in Bradenton, Florida. General manager
John McHale said, "From now on, fans will be able to sit anywhere
in the park regardless of race. We insisted on this to the city officials
of Bradenton and they told us that we could run the park as we see
fit. We also have removed the COLORED and WHITE signs on the
washrooms and at the gates and the ticket windows.'"

It wasn't very many years ago that the Dodgers, staying in Chicago at the Edgewater Beach Hotel a few miles north of the city proper on Lake Shore Drive, had to make separate housing arrangements for all their Negro players. The ball club didn't like the situation but it was hardly peculiar to Chicago and they didn't see what they could do about it. Then, when Jackie Robinson was one of the elder statesmen of the club and his teammates included Roy Campanella and Don Newcombe, the management of the hotel told Lee Scott, the Dodgers' traveling secretary, that it would be all right for the colored ballplayers to stay at the hotel with everybody else if they would agree to stay out of the public rooms—that is, not to linger in the lobby, eat in the dining rooms, drink in the bars or do anything except go directly to and from their rooms. They could have food delivered to them by room service, but except for that they would be given nothing except sleeping space. Campanella, the easygoing man, said no, he thought not, if they didn't want to take him on the same terms that applied to the white ballplayers, he would rather stay somewhere else. Newcombe said he guessed he would do whatever Campy did. Robinson, the rebel, the angry man, thought it over and said, well, he figured it was a step in the right direction, and he would go along with it. In the end, Campanella and Newcombe went along with it too, and a few months later they got their reward. Jackie's wife, Rae, was making a western trip with him, and secretary Scott had booked the couple into a double room at the Edgewater Beach. Obeying the gentleman's agreement he had entered into with the hotel, Jack took Rae out to dinner in a Chicago restaurant the first night of their stay and made sure that they were very scarce around the hotel. "I see Mrs. Robinson is here with Jackie," the hotel manager said to Lee Scott the next day. "I wish you'd tell Jack we'd be very pleased to have them eat in the dining room any time they want—and for that matter why don't you tell all the boys, Campy and Newcombe too, that

that goes for them, too, all the time." So baseball took another purposeful step forward in the national surge toward equality for all.

I'm reminded of another incident that struck me at the time as being meaningful despite its relative unimportance. Eight people, four men interested in baseball and their wives, were having dinner at Dinty Moore's restaurant on 46th Street just off Broadway in New York City a few years ago. While they were eating, a lady came table-hopping across from the other side of the room and extended an eager hand to Elston Howard. "You *are* Elston Howard, aren't you?" she said hopefully. And when Ellie acknowledged that he was, she bubbled on. "I've always wanted to meet you. I've admired you ever since you came up with the Yankees. I think you're a wonderful ballplayer and I'd be terribly grateful if you would sign this menu for me so I can bring it home to my son. He lives and dies with the Yankees and he's going to be *so* jealous when he hears I actually met you." It was nice to see a fine fellow like Ellie singled out for such effusive attention in a restaurant frequented by the biggest names in the entertainment and sports worlds. It was even more impressive when you considered that sitting quietly at the other end of the table, happily chewing his steak, was a pretty good ballplayer named Yogi Berra.

It's true, I think, that sports people in general pay very little attention to the color of a man's skin. They are trained from childhood to consider only performance in evaluating a fellow or rival athlete. What matters to a baseball man is how you can hit, field, run and throw. The great scout, like Branch Rickey or Paul Krichell or Tom Greenwade, knows that no race or nationality has a patent on the qualities that make a ballplayer. Stan Musial is Polish, Hank Greenberg is a Jew, Sandy Koufax is a Greek and a Jew, Joe DiMaggio is an Italian—and so it goes. But, although not more than a bare handful of baseball men had to be convinced, an important benefit of the integration of the major leagues was the unmistakable demonstration to the public at large of the falsity of the old wives' tales that Negro athletes were showboats, front-runners, unreliable in the clutch. When Jackie Robinson did the kind of thing he did on the last day of the 1951 season, it was a dramatically taught national lesson.

That was the year the Giants had come from 13½ games back in the middle of August to challenge the Dodgers for the pennant in the dying days of the race. On Sunday, September 30, a day which began with them tied for first place with the Giants, the Dodgers played the Phillies in Philadelphia. Before the fifth inning of their game was over, they knew from the scoreboard that the Giants had beaten the Braves in Boston, 3–2, for their 37th victory in their last 44 games. The Dodgers had to win to stay alive, but their chances looked poor when the Phillies scored two runs in the last of the fifth to take an 8–5 lead. They didn't give up, though. In the top of the eighth they put together singles by Gil Hodges, Billy Cox and Carl Furillo, and a double by Rube Walker, for the three runs they needed to tie. That was the way it stood through the 11th inning. The fireworks started when the Phillies came to bat in the 12th.

Each team had its best pitcher in there by then, Robin Roberts for the Phillies and Don Newcombe for the Dodgers. Roberts drew a base on balls to open the Philadelphia half of the 12th, and when Newcombe threw late to second trying to force Roberts on Eddie Pellagrini's bunt, all hands were safe. Things looked a little better for the Dodgers when Richie Ashburn forced Pellagrini at second and Newcombe struck out Del Ennis, but it seemed to be all over when first baseman Eddie Waitkus lashed a wickedly twisting, low line drive that seemed surely headed for the open reaches of center field. But Robinson, playing second base for Brooklyn, hurled himself to his right, dived frantically for the ball and made an incredible stop, holding on to the ball even though he hit the ground so hard that all the wind was knocked out of him and his right elbow was jammed into his stomach so forcibly that he felt dazed and sick. Doc Wendler, the Brooklyn trainer, stretched Jackie out full length on the dugout bench and worked over him feverishly as the Dodgers went out meekly in their half of the 13th. Jackie was pretty far gone, though, and not even Wendler's wad of ammonia-soaked cotton was able to rouse him from his exhaustion. Robinson's double-play partner and best friend on the ball club, Peewee Reese, stood at the top of the dugout steps and looked down at him. "Come on, Jackie," he said softly, "we need you now, boy." When Doc Wendler looked at him questioningly, and then looked around for manager Charlie Dressen, Reese said firmly, "Never mind, Doc. Just push him up here. He'll be all right as soon as he gets out on the ball field."

"I'm not sure I can do anything," Jackie said, still half in a fog.

"If you can't," Reese said, "I don't know who can."

So the Dodgers held the Phillies in the 13th, and in the top of the 14th inning, with two out and nobody on base, a tired second base-man named Jackie Robinson hit a home run over the left-field fence to win the ball game. He says himself it was the best game he ever played. Watching it, it would have been hard for even the most un-reconstructed rebel of them all to argue that "you can't trust them Nigras when the going gets tough." Jackie Robinson, like Willie Mays who came after him, was always at his best when things got really tough. It's the mark of a true champion to do the kind of thing Robinson did in Philadelphia that day in 1951 and the kind of thing he did against the Yankees at Ebbets Field in Brooklyn during the World Series of 1956.

Don Larsen's incredible Perfect Game had put the Yankees ahead, three games to two, in the Series when the ancient rivals went back across the river to the bandbox Brooklyn ball park for the last two games—if two games would be needed to settle it. For nine innings nobody could do anything against the strong pitching of the Yan-kees' Bob Turley and the Dodgers' Clem Labine. In the 10th, though, with two on and two out, Jackie Robinson came up for

Brooklyn. Jack was going on thirty-eight years old that October, and he was no longer the consistent hitter he had been a few years before. Some of the old-timers in the press box wondered, as Jack got up from his crouch in the on-deck circle, if manager Walter Alston would send in a younger man to hit for him. But it was Jackie Robinson, a little heavier, a lot grayer, and undeniably older than the exciting rookie who had made baseball history in 1947, who walked out to the plate and took up his familiar pigeon-toed stance. It was Jackie Robinson who slashed at one of Bob Turley's pitches and whacked the ball high and far over the head of Yankee left fielder Enos Slaughter, off the Ebbets Field wall, the ball bounding happily back onto the green grass of the outfield as the run came home and the Dodgers won it, 1–0.

Dick Young, one of the best reporters ever to cover the baseball beat, asked Alston after the game if he had thought of putting in a pinch hitter for Robinson. "No," Alston said in his quiet way, "I never did. If I had to win it or lose it with one man, I couldn't ask for anybody better than Jack."

It seems unbelievable today that in 1947 a substantial part of the roster of the St. Louis Cardinals proposed to strike rather than play against a Brooklyn Dodger lineup including the Negro Jackie Robinson. The first game scheduled between the two clubs was set for May 6, and the Cardinal dissidents planned to arrange matters so that their club would not be able to field a team that day. Later in the season, they thought, it would be easy enough to call a general strike of all National League players in protest against the presence of a Negro player in the league. All their plans were ruined because a brave president of the National League, Ford Frick, and an alert and fearless sports editor, Stanley Woodward of the New York *Herald Tribune*, heard of their plans and moved resolutely to frustrate them. Frick moved first, and he moved fast; he took care of the immediate threat. Woodward publicized it and ridiculed it and thereby eliminated the threat for all time.

The heart of Woodward's prize-winning journalistic coup was his report of what Frick told the St. Louis ballplayers:

"If you do this you will be suspended from the league. You will find that the friends you think you have in the press box will not support you, that you will be outcasts. I do not care if half the league strikes. Those who do it will encounter quick retribution. All will be suspended and I don't care if it wrecks the National League for five years. This is the United States of America and one citizen has as much right to play as another. The National League will go down the line with Robinson whatever the consequences. You will find if you go through with your intention that you have been guilty of complete madness."

It is more believable that only a few years ago a particularly gifted sportswriter, Roger Kahn, should have written this about Jackie Robinson as the symbol of the Negro in baseball:

Jackie Robinson will speak his mind. This American Negro, born in Georgia, bred in California, loved and hated everywhere, will not sit in the back of a bus or call all white men "Mister." He does not drawl his words and he isn't afraid of ghosts and he isn't ashamed of his skin and he never says, "Yowsah, boss." This American Negro, this dark symbol of enlightenment, is proud and educated and sensitive and indiscreet and hot-tempered and warm-hearted. Those who do not know Robinson will call him "troublemaker." Those who do not understand him will call him "popoff guy." Perhaps both terms are right. Robinson has made trouble for bigots, more trouble than they could handle.

Branch Rickey, who supposedly is the finest scout in baseball history, chose Robinson with wisdom that borders upon clairvoyance, to right a single wrong. Robinson had the playing ability to become a super-star, plus the intelligence to understand the significance of his role. He had the fighting temperament to wring the most from his ability and he had the self control to keep his temper in check.

It is even more readily believable that only a few years ago a battery of authorities on the subject, including tennis champion

Althea Gibson, football hero Buddy Young, major-league baseball's Larry Doby (the first Negro ever to play in the American League), Negro sportswriter Sam Lacy of Baltimore, and Jackie Robinson should have pooled their ideas in a round-table discussion arranged by a national magazine to consider the subject: "The Negro in American Sport." I've always thought that Larry Doby's opening remarks to the group were particularly effective:

"I think we've had great success," Larry said, "but we've still got a long way to go, and it's going to be a matter of education. . . . If you don't know enough, you're going to be disillusioned. In school, they tell you this is a free country, you can go where you want to go and do what you want to do. . . . But, hell, you go down South and you can't go where you want to go. For instance, even up north, all of a sudden I'm with Cleveland, I want to ride in a cab and a guy says you can't ride in this cab. They didn't tell me that in school. By the same token, they never had any Negro history in school, and I think they should. So all right, I can't ride in a cab, and here I am facing reality. First of all, I get mad at the guy, and that may not be the proper thing to do. It may not be his fault. How are you going to cope with this except through education?"

"Education is important," Jackie Robinson said skeptically, "but it's only part of the answer. Some people will never change voluntarily. They'll always be bigoted. You can't wait for them to change. That would be like a man with somebody's foot on his throat waiting until he was choked to death. You have to make some moves yourself."

That led to an interesting point about the Negro athlete's dilemma when he is confronted with an opportunity to move into the white man's world, an opportunity he knows would never have come his way if it hadn't been for his special status as a celebrity. "Now that you're taking up golf," Althea was asked, "would you accept an invitation to play at a white golf club if you knew it wasn't open to other Negroes?" "Certainly I would," Althea said quickly. "If they accepted me on the basis of my ability, then sooner or later they would accept others on the basis of their ability regardless of race."

"There was a time," Robinson said thoughtfully, "when I would have disagreed violently on that. I wouldn't have considered going to a club where other Negroes weren't welcome. But I've talked to a lot of people about it, people I respect, and they've all said, 'Jackie, you've got to go. If you don't, how will we ever be able to get there? Somebody has to be first.' "

The meeting took up, too, the question you often hear raised by wary baseball men about the possibility that the tremendously skillful Negro players will end up "taking over" the game. The question was put, that day, directly to Larry Doby, the old Cleveland Indian. "They tell me this is a free country," Larry said, repeating his favorite phrase. "If the Negroes have more ability, they should get the chance to show it. Believe me, if the Negro is better than the other fellow, and I think he has to be twice as good to get there, it's a God-given ability. It won't be a problem, not in San Francisco or anywhere else, no matter how many Negroes any one team has. Everybody loves a winner. If you have nine Negroes on a ball club, and they're winning, the people will love them."

Robinson's observation was both temperate, I thought, and wise. "I don't think the day will ever come," he said, "when the Negro will dominate baseball. The fact that a man is a Negro doesn't make him a better ballplayer than the white man. Only ten per cent of the country's population is Negro, and there are so many young men who want to play ball that ten per cent of the total population is not going to take over. Certain clubs may have a lot of Negro players now, but you have to remember that times have changed and all of the ball clubs are scouting Negro prospects regularly these days. No one team is going to end up with most of them . . .

it will simply be a normal allotment all around. . . . On the other hand, I don't agree that a Negro ballplayer has to be twice as good as a white one to make the majors. Like I said, times have changed."

In the summer of 1963 times had changed enough for the Commissioner of Baseball, Ford Frick, to tell a committee of the United States Senate holding hearings on President John F. Kennedy's proposals for a new civil rights bill that "baseball is a very model of integration." The Commissioner forthrightly told the senators that "baseball has paid a price for this in the loss of certain cities that otherwise might be fielding a team today." He was referring specifically to Birmingham, Montgomery, Shreveport and New Orleans, which dropped out of Organized Baseball rather than accept integration on the ball field. But he pointed out that other southern cities, including Chattanooga, Atlanta and Little Rock, had come back to the fold and were experiencing no difficulty with integrated teams. He put on the record a letter from Ray Winder, general manager of the Arkansas Travelers in Little Rock, which said in part:

We quietly integrated on April 16, 1963. A crowd of 6,966, including several hundred Negroes, attended. There was no trouble, no commotion, no complaints. There was one old fellow who carried a sign protesting the first night. But he gave up the second night of the season. Our Negro players are popular with the fans. They came here in fear, but a large group of white fans met the team on their arrival here and took them on a tour of the city. They are very much at home now. We sold $114,330 worth of pre-season tickets to 90 cities outside Little Rock itself. Integration in Little Rock has been smooth.

Senator John O. Pastore of Rhode Island, who obviously knew the answer to his question, asked Commissioner Frick, "Who threw out the first ball to open the season in Little Rock?"

Frick grinned. "Governor Orval E. Faubus," he said. He was plainly pleased that baseball had been able to do what all the might of the federal government had not been able to do—get Governor Faubus to endorse a project involving integration of the races.

Senator Warren G. Magnuson of Washington, the chairman of the committee, asked the Commissioner how many Negroes there were in Organized Baseball. Frick's answer was as eloquent a statement of baseball's position as I've ever come across. "I haven't any idea," he said. "I don't think anybody does. We don't keep records on that. We keep batting averages, fielding averages, pitching records and other statistics, birth dates and so forth, but we don't keep records on color or religion. We have no figures on how many players are black, white or yellow because they are selected on the basis of whether they can pitch, hit or play second base."

What it all means to the country, it seems to me, is that baseball not only has been willing to make the great experiment but has gone on to prove that it can work. In doing so it has earned for all time the right to call itself the national game.

Chapter 8

Mantle? I know he shouldn't play so much when
he's hurt, but maybe the other pitcher doesn't
know it. Just having him in there makes the
lineup look stronger. It doesn't look the
same without him.—GIL MCDOUGALD

YOU have to give consideration to several different
theories when you look for the reason why the Yankees seem to win
the championship of the American League every year and the
championship of the world on an average of four years out of
every five.

There is the never-say-die theory, sometimes said to be the result
of the teachings of such hard-nosed managers as Joe McCarthy,
Casey Stengel and Ralph Houk, men who have in common the attitude that Yankees aren't supposed to lose very often and never
submissively. A friend of mine who was down on the field when the
Yankees were in Comiskey Park, Chicago, playing out the tag end
of the 1959 season, the year they lost the pennant to the White Sox,
tells a story that illustrates this theory. Hank Bauer swung hard at
a third strike and missed it and a White Sox fan sitting in a box
behind home plate yelled at him, "Don't take it so hard, Bauer!
Remember the law of averages. Even the Yankees have to lose some-

100

time!" My friend reports that Hank turned around as he walked back to the dugout and called back, over his shoulder, "Yeah, but there's no law that says you have to like it."

There is the bench theory, which says that the Yankees win because they always have the best bench in baseball. When one man gets hurt or slumps, the manager just leans back and, as Jimmy Dykes once said sarcastically, pushes a button, and the necessary replacement leaps gracefully into the breach and does what has to be done. The believers in the bench theory had a field day during the 1963 season which saw Mickey Mantle sit out a good part of the season, Roger Maris out for a long stretch in mid-season, and practically every regular on the club hurt or sick at different times. There were only nine times all year when the entire "varsity" outfield, Mantle, Maris and Tommy Tresh, was able to play as a unit. But for substitutes the Yankees could call on the likes of Hector Lopez, potential Hall of Famer Yogi Berra, and John Blanchard. Even the rinkydinks, or, as the ballplayers call them, the scrubinis, Harry Bright, Jack Reed and Phil Linz, came through day after day. Elston Howard explained it as well as anybody when he said, "This is a team, and it stands up. No matter who you put in there, things happen."

Then there is the money theory, which says with a shrug that these guys just can't be beaten when they smell that World Series money. Jimmy Breslin of the New York *Herald Tribune* is a believer in the money theory. "The thing that makes the Yankees win no matter who seems to be in there," he said, "is The Other Check. The Other Check comes in the mail in October, and it is a big one, because it is from the World Series, and if you are a baseball player in Yankee Stadium, The Other Check is supposed to be automatic every year. You step in and help to get the thing, or you go and play someplace else." To humanize his theory, Jimmy told about an incident he had witnessed at Fort Lauderdale in spring camp. "Frank Crosetti, the coach, stood at home plate and hit ground balls to the infield," he said. "On one of them, Joe Pepitone picked up the shot at first, threw to second, then shuffled back toward first to take the return throw. Crosetti let out a squawk, 'Touch the bag!' he yelled. 'You touch the bag every time!' The Crow shook his head. 'They get into bad habits doing things that way,' he said. 'They get sloppy. And up here, when they get sloppy, they're messing around with my money.' "

There is nothing wrong with any of these theories. The Yankees do play to win, they don't believe in losing submissively, they do manage to put together a strong bench year after year and thus protect themselves against the inevitable injuries, and they do respond to the lure of money because they are professionals and this is how they make a living. Furthermore, as young Yankees they have observed the older Yankees and have seen what success and the money it brings can provide in the way of the good life, and understandably they want to get in on it. It is also true that with the Yankees you not only touch the bag every time in practice, you stamp on it, because the Yankees think the little things are important and they don't believe in taking any chances. I subscribe, in part, to all of these theories but I would have to add two others.

The first is that the Yankees win not because they have more money than the other clubs but because they have organization and tradition. When it comes to money, I imagine that the fine man who owns the Boston Red Sox, Tom Yawkey, himself has more money than both the Yankee owners put together, but he has been able to win only one pennant. Phil Wrigley has all the money in the world but his Chicago Cubs haven't done very well for a long time. The Yankees obtain their ballplayers, develop them, and win pennants with them through superior organization, and through tradition and the pride that tradition instills in all hands. Run down the Yankees' starting lineup for 1963 and try to find a big bonus player. You can't. The Dodgers are supposed to have spent $3,000,000 for bonus players in three years; the Yankees have never done anything like that. But the Yankees were one of the first professional teams to develop the kind of tradition that plays so great a part in the success of the finest college teams. Tradition doesn't make you a great ballplayer but it does bring out the best that is in you. It gives you pride, and confidence. It makes you care. With the Yankees, you have to care or you don't stay around very long. This tradition of one hundred percent effort at all times is enforced not only by the manager and the coaches, but by the older players, who are quick to jack up a backslider. It's a tradition that says it is a proud thing to be a Yankee. It's a tradition that produces pennants.

The other theory I want to add is an obvious one. For a very long time now the Yankee ball club has been led by a bellwether who was a genuine, 14-karat superstar. First there was Babe Ruth (who had his Lou Gehrig), then there was Joe DiMaggio (who had his Tommy Henrich, and Yogi Berra too), and now there is Mickey Mantle (who had Yogi Berra first and now has Roger Maris). The big club has always had a big man to show the way, and ever since 1952 the man has been Mickey Charles Mantle.

You hear, as the seasons go by, about so many "can't miss" rookies who are going to be "another DiMaggio" or "another Williams" or "another Musial" that you tend as you get older and more experienced to be almost excessively suspicious of the young player whose arrival on the scene is heralded by loud blasts of the publicity department's trumpets. It was that way for a lot of people with Mantle. Nobody, they figured, could be as good as they said this kid was. They shrugged off as prejudiced and wishful thinking what Tom Greenwade, the scout, said about him: "Now I know how Paul Krichell felt when he first saw Lou Gehrig. He told me once that the first time he saw him he knew this was it. He knew that as a scout he'd never have another moment like it. I felt the same way when I first saw Mickey Mantle. He's got to be one of the game's all-time greats."

"The fastest man in baseball going down to first base."

"Hits with destructive power to all fields. The greatest switch-hitter since Frank Frisch, and hits a much longer ball."

That was the kind of thing the newspapermen kept writing about Mickey in the spring of 1951 as the Yankees, who had exchanged training bases for a year with the Giants, went through their workouts and their exhibition games in Phoenix, Arizona. Back home there were skeptics who wondered if it wasn't all a phony buildup designed to make the fans forget that Joe DiMaggio was getting toward the end of the line and indeed already had said he would hang up his spikes after this season. But then Branch Rickey handed down The Word on Mantle: "I've been looking for ballplayers for a long time and this boy is the finest prospect I've ever seen. He's my ideal rookie. He's the kind of boy I've always dreamed of finding but never have. He has that flawless, level swing, and the fastest break from the plate I've ever seen."

Rickey even went so far as to stick a note in Dan Topping's pocket at one spring game telling the co-owner of the Yankees, "With this I make my official bid to buy Mickey Mantle for the Pirates. Name your own price, but for goodness sake, be reasonable." Topping read the note and laughed. "You can have him for Ralph Kiner," he said, "if you'll throw in half a million dollars to sweeten the deal." But Topping was only kidding. Not even Kiner the home-run hitter and a satchel filled with $500,000 could have bought Mickey Mantle that spring or any spring since. The Yankees have never been sorry that they held on to Mickey for dear life—bad legs, bad knees, bad shoulder, bad cartilages and all. With Mickey they won 11 American League pennants in the 13 seasons from 1951 through 1963. With Mickey, acknowledged to be the number one player in the game whenever he was even reasonably healthy, they remained the number one team.

We all have so many different impressions and memories of Mickey Mantle, who has not always been the same person or even the same ballplayer from year to year, that it isn't easy to tell anyone exactly what you think of Mick. We have known a whole lot of different Mickeys. Beginning, of course, with the bashful kid at

Phoenix in 1951. You couldn't get a word out of that Mickey with a can opener. One writer broke through a little bit by finding a subject that interested him. "I hope you're not going to ask me a whole lot of questions," Mickey said when the writer sat down with him. "I'm no good at answering questions." That was a pretty long speech for Mantle right there. But the writer didn't back off. He just said, "Who's your favorite jazz musician?" Mickey grunted. "Don't like jazz," he said. "Well," the writer wanted to know, "what kind of music do you like?" "Hillbilly," Mickey said. "You do? I'll bet you like Red Foley then." Mickey's face lit up. "Sure do." He grinned. "I like the way he sings."

Come to think of it, on that score, Mickey hasn't changed very much. As anybody who spends much time hanging around the Yankee clubhouse knows, Mickey still likes hillbilly music.

To understand Mickey at all you have to understand his background. He comes from Commerce, Oklahoma, a little town of about 3,000 people, most of whom hack a hard living out of the lead and zinc mines that honeycomb the ground underneath the streets of the town. Mickey's father, Elven, whose friends called him Mutt, was a foreman in the mines. He also was devoted to baseball, played it every chance he got and followed the big-league scores religiously. His favorite ballplayer was Mickey Cochrane, the great catcher of the Athletics and later player-manager of the Tigers. Elven's first child, a boy, was born on October 30, 1931, just a few weeks after the World Series in which the Cardinals, with Pepper Martin stealing everything but Cochrane's glove, had beaten the A's in seven games. Bad Series or no bad Series, Elven named the boy Mickey. Mickey is his real name, not a nickname.

He grew up, in that remote northeast corner of Oklahoma, loving baseball and playing it for hours at a time, first with his father, his grandfather Charles Mantle from whom he took his middle name, and his Uncle Emmett, Elven's younger brother. Actually, Mickey didn't play the game half as much as he practiced it. Mutt

Mantle was bound and determined that the boy was going to be a big-league baseball player, and he didn't spare the discipline in getting him ready for it. It was Mutt's idea that Mickey would be better equipped for the big leagues if he hit from both sides of the plate—that is, batted right-handed against left-handed pitching and left-handed against right-handed pitching. Fortunately for the Mantle back-yard baseball school, Grandpa was a righty and Mutt was a lefty. Mickey didn't do so well batting left-handed in the beginning, but after a while he improved, and by the time he was playing for his high school team it was second nature to him to "turn around" at the plate. Many a baseball man has argued that he would be a better hitter if he stuck to a right-handed stance, the one that is more natural for him, and even Mickey agrees that he can generate more power swinging right-handed. But Mickey is unwilling to give up the advantage he possesses in being able to switch from one side to the other depending upon the contours of the ball park he happens to be in and the kind of pitcher he happens to be facing. Too many major-league parks, including Yankee Stadium, are friendly to the left-handed hitter and hostile to the righty. Mickey's father knew what he was doing.

"I'll tell you one thing," Tom Greenwade told Mutt Mantle when he signed young Mickey to a Yankee contract, "you know more baseball than the father of any kid I ever signed." That's a testimonial Mickey is proud of; he thought the world of his father. Mutt Mantle masterminded every step of Mickey's advancement into professional baseball, from catcher for the Douthat, Oklahoma, team in the Pee Wee League to shortstop for Commerce High and the Baxter Springs (Kansas) Whiz Kids in the American Legion Junior Baseball League. After that it was Independence in the Kansas-Oklahoma-Missouri League (Class D), Joplin in the Western Association (Class C), and the New York Yankees of the American League (the highest class there is). Mutt had done his job well.

Tom Greenwade saw Mickey play only three or four ball games before he asked Mutt to sign a contract for him. But they were

enough. Baseball scouts don't expect kid prospects to be polished
fielders, so it didn't bother Greenwade that young Mantle tended to
surround a ground ball instead of picking it up cleanly in his glove.
What mattered to this weather-beaten ivory-hunter was the way
the boy could run, hit and throw. Those are the things, the scouts
will tell you, that can't be taught. You can always teach a boy how
to field adequately enough to keep from getting hurt. Even Rudy
York, "part Indian and part first baseman," made the grade. There
wasn't a shred of doubt in Greenwade's mind that he had picked up
a diamond in the rough.

He picked him up cheaply, too, signing him the night Mickey was
supposed to attend his high school graduation exercises. Instead, he
was in Coffeyville, Kansas, the town where the Dalton gang was shot
to pieces trying to rob the local bank. The principal of the high
school had given him his diploma in advance that afternoon, which
was all right with Mickey and his father because it meant they
didn't have to worry about getting him a new blue suit for the occasion, and the Whiz Kids were playing the Coffeyville entry in the
Ban Johnson League. Before the game, while Mickey and his high
school coach, John Lingo, were having a hamburger and french
fried potatoes in a Coffeyville diner, Mutt and Greenwade talked
business. "I can give him a Class D contract for $140 a month,"
Greenwade said. There wasn't anything in the world that Mutt
wanted more than he wanted that Yankee contract for his son, but
he also knew that Mickey had to make ends meet when he left home.
"That doesn't seem like much money," he said cautiously. "I could
get him ninety cents an hour in the mines and he can pick up a
couple of semipro games a week for ten or fifteen dollars apiece. The
kind of money you're talking about, the kid's got to work all winter
in the mines anyway. I don't know. It don't seem like much."

Greenwade got out his pencil and started figuring. After a while
he said, "A thousand dollar bonus, then, okay?" Mutt Mantle said
okay and the deal was made. The Yankees owned the contract of a
million-dollar ballplayer, and Mickey Mantle was on his way to

fame and wealth. He did work in the mines, as an electrician's helper in his father's pit, the Blue Goose No. 1, for the next two winters, because even when his salary at Joplin was raised to $250 a month, he didn't have much left over at the end of the baseball season. He had to buy clothes, he had to pay for his room and board when the ball club was at home, he had to have money for the western movies he liked so much, and he had to send some money home to his mother every month. But once his two-year stay in the minors was over, and he became a Yankee, his money problem disappeared quickly. In his first couple of seasons with the Yankees he probably made more money out of endorsements, testimonials and paid appearances than he did in salary. But later, when he was firmly established not as the new DiMaggio but as the original and guaranteed-one-of-a-kind Mickey Mantle, the money poured in like a spring flood.

The innocent small-town boy from out west had to grow up fast. He did it the hard way. When he first came to New York in April, 1951, a fast-talking Broadway agent persuaded him to sign a contract covering all of his outside activities. The agent swore that the contract would be worth $50,000 a year to Mickey and made it sound reasonable that all fees should be split 50–50 between Mickey and him. The going rate for the services of such an agent—and useful services they are—is ten per cent, but Mickey had no way of knowing it. He didn't even have a lawyer represent him in the deal because, the agent pointed out, he already had one, so why waste money? It took the Yankees over a year and many hours of expensive work by the club's legal staff to get Mickey out of that one. Since then the kid from Commerce has learned how to take care of himself in the Madison Avenue clinches.

Most important, he has learned how to take care of himself on the ball fields of the American League, and even though Mickey is a natural ballplayer if there ever was such a thing, that was no easier than learning his way around the big city. The Old Professor, Casey Stengel, was his chief instructor, of course, with Tommy Henrich, in the beginning, a close second. Mickey first met Stengel at the Yankees' special school for rookies at Phoenix in February of 1950. The school didn't last long because Branch Rickey complained to Commissioner Happy Chandler that, with nine Yankee ballplayers joining the manager and the coaches on the "faculty," it came pretty close to violating the rule against starting spring training before March 1. But it lasted long enough for Stengel to watch eighteen-year-old Mickey win a footrace among the "students" and to give him a few thousand words of advice in his best Stengelese. "If you learned to run like that chasin' them jackrabbits back home," Casey, an old settler from Kansas, said, "just be sure and keep it up because we can use young fellers like you who can run like that on the Yankees and it won't hurt you none pickin' up them leg hits to push up your average, neither." Casey drew a breath and came a little closer to basic English. "You keep on practicin' everything these men are tellin' you," he said, "and I'll see you here in Phoenix again next spring when we bring the Yankees out here, and maybe you and me can have some fun together."

It was more than fun that the old man and the boy had in March and April of 1951, it was a circus. Baseball had seen big buildups for rookies before, most recently for the Giants' Clint Hartung, the Hondo Hurricane, who was supposed to be Frank Merriwell, Incorporated, when he arrived at the Polo Grounds in 1947, blown in by a gale of publicity that claimed he could hit like Mel Ott and pitch like Bob Feller. Unhappily for the Giants it turned out that he hit like Bob Feller and pitched like Mel Ott. So the writers as well as the fans were good-naturedly dubious about this new phenomenon; he would have to show them. Well, Mickey Mantle showed them. If you were a New York, Chicago or Los Angeles columnist coming upon the camp scene a few weeks after Mickey had begun to monopolize all the headlines back home, you were professionally skeptical. Surely the boys, even the tough old-timers like Dan Daniel of New York, Gordon Cobbledick of Cleveland and Warren Brown of Chicago, must be letting the sun get to them to write the kind of raves they had been filing at the Western Union office about this kid. You would be likely to remind the early birds at the camp about the ancient spring training joke about the rookie whose letters home to mother were one long story of success and hope until, finally, he sat down and wrote, "I'll be home soon, Mom, the pitchers started throwing curves today." But, two days later, you would have caught the Mickey Mantle virus and you would have become a true believer. Jack Orr put it all down in a piece he wrote late that spring for the long-gone New York *Compass*:

Some of us were kicking it around in a compartment on the Yankee train speeding through Texas. We worked over a couple of subjects but, as always, we got back to the same old one. It was bedtime when somebody said, "Cripes, we've been going for three hours and we haven't talked about anything except Mickey Mantle." The man was right. And we weren't the only ones talking about the kid's fabulous showing this spring.

"Sometimes I don't know," one man said, "if I'd rather see him bunt or hit a homer. Sometimes I'd rather see him get up left-handed, and then I see him hit one four miles the other way and I prefer that."

"I get mad if a pitcher walks him," another man said.

What it comes down to is this. Those of us who have been beating the drums for Mantle are hoping he makes it to the Stadium just to prove that we haven't lost our marbles completely.

George Weiss, the man in the front office, didn't think that, good as he plainly was, Mickey ought to stay with the Yankees. He preferred sending him out for one more year of seasoning with the top farm club of the chain, Kansas City. Casey Stengel, the man in the dugout, began by more or less agreeing with Weiss, then came around to the newspapermen's point of view, which was pretty much that the kid was better already than most major-leaguers, so why not let him learn his trade with the big boys? If it didn't hurt Mel Ott, they reasoned, why should it hurt Mantle? In the end, Casey and the newspapermen won out, and when the Yankees pulled into New York for their annual spring exhibition series with the Dodgers on the eve of the opening of the regular season, the young man they were already beginning to call The Switcher was still there. The first game of the series was played at Ebbets Field and before the game Casey sat in the dugout and talked about walking out into the right-field corner with Mickey during batting practice and showing him how to play the famous fence. "I told him Carl Furillo plays carom shots off this fence like a pool player," Casey said, "and I also told him that I played it myself for six years when I was with the Dodgers and I never had no trouble with it. And you know, I don't think the kid believed me? I think he thinks I was born at the age of sixty and immediately became the manager of the Yankees."

Mickey took some razzing from the Brooklyn fans when he produced only one single in that first game, but in the second game of the series he came through with a home run and three singles, and nobody even thought about giving him the Ebbets Field raspberry. They just sat there wishing he were a Dodger, a wish they were to renew year after year on many a painful fall afternoon during World Series time.

The fancy .402 batting average Mantle had fashioned in spring training, the 41 hits, the 31 runs batted in, the 9 home runs, meant nothing once the Yankees decided to keep him and he reported to Yankee Stadium for the Opening Day game on Tuesday afternoon, April 17, 1951. Now they would be playing for keeps, the pitchers would be throwing their best curves, the old pros would be in the lineup and the kids who had come up for what the ballplayers call "a cup of coffee" would be on their way back to the minors. But wearing the pin-striped uniform of Babe Ruth, Lou Gehrig and Bill Dickey, playing alongside Joe DiMaggio in the Yankee outfield, in the position that was Ruth's own, was Mickey Charles Mantle, former shortstop for Joplin, Missouri, and now, they were saying in the press box and in the stands, the heir apparent to the great Joe D. himself. The Yankees had never had a ballplayer come from so far down the organization ladder to make their club. The man who ran the store still didn't think he should be there. There were thousands of fans who thought the whole thing was a publicity hoax that quickly would be exposed and would end with the kid back in Joplin where he belonged. It wasn't a comfortable spot that Mickey was on.

But, as happens to all young ballplayers, once the game began Mickey forgot about the awe he had felt when he first walked into the expensively appointed dressing quarters of the world champion Yankees, he forgot about the 44,860 people in the huge triple-decked Stadium, he forgot about the winking television cameras and the hundreds of reporters massed in the big press box behind home plate, he forgot about everything except the pitch and the swing of the bat, the ball whooshing in to the plate to be hit or hanging briefly in the blue outfield sky to be caught. "At first," Mickey said honestly, "I was scared silly. I was afraid I'd bump into DiMaggio and make a fool out of myself. I was afraid I'd not only strike out but I'd miss the ball by a mile. But then the game started and everything was all right. I was too busy to worry."

Casey Stengel's batting order that day had Jackie Jensen in left field, Phil Rizzuto at shortstop, Mantle in right field, Joe DiMaggio in center, Yogi Berra catching, Johnny Mize at first base, Billy Johnson at third, Jerry Coleman at second, and Vic Raschi pitching. His first time up, Mickey went out on an easy grounder to second baseman Bobby Doerr. The second time, he raised a pop fly to shortstop Vernon Stephens. Then, in the sixth inning, with Jensen on third and Rizzuto on first, he drove a single through the left side of the infield for his first major-league hit and his first run batted in. He didn't hit his first major-league home run until May 1 in Chicago, but he kept his batting average around .300 as the May 15 cutdown date came and went and the Yankees kept him on the roster without comment. It looked as though he had it made. Even the draft board in Miami, Oklahoma, which seemed to want to examine him all over again every time he hit another home run, reaffirmed for the third time that his history of osteomyelitis in the

right leg made him automatically unacceptable for military service,
so Mickey knew where he stood there, too. His girl friend back
home, Merlyn Johnson, from nearby Picher, who had been a drum
majorette for Picher High when Mickey was going to Commerce
High, had agreed to marry him when the season was over if they
both still thought it was a good idea then. Mickey didn't think he
could ask for much more. But May turned out to be a long month,
and before it was over he was up to his neck in misery.

It didn't happen all at once. Even when it all came to a head
Mickey had more hits to his credit than all but two of the Yankees,
Rizzuto and Berra, and only Berra had batted in more runs. But
whether it was the relentless publicity, the constant demands on his
time, his lack of experience in the major leagues, or, more likely,
simply his lack of maturity, Mickey began to come apart at the
seams. There was a doubleheader with the Red Sox at Boston on
Memorial Day in which Mickey struck out five times in a row as
the Yankees lost both games. After the fifth strikeout he stormed
into the dugout, rushed up to the water cooler and kicked it savagely. "Son," Stengel told him with what was for him unusual gentleness, "that water cooler ain't strikin' you out." It was too much
for Mickey; he probably could have taken a bawling out better. He
sat down on the bench and cried. "You better take me out of there
and put in somebody who can hit," he said in a shaking voice. Casey
did, and two weeks later he went a step further and sent Mickey
down to Kansas City. With Mickey, Casey forwarded these instructions to George Selkirk, the Kansas City manager:

"Please play Mantle in center field, and play him every day."

Casey didn't want anybody, Mantle, Selkirk, the newspapermen
or the other Yankees, to have any doubts about his future plans for
Mantle. Mickey was going to play center field for the Yankees in
1952 and for a long time to come. Mickey understood what was
going on, and even if he didn't rejoice over the trip to Kansas City,
he offered no complaints. "It's all right with me," he said soberly.
"I'd rather play every day down there than just sit on the bench up

here. Nobody has to tell me I've got an awful lot to learn about hitting and outfielding."

"He'll be back," Casey told the press. "I haven't quit on the boy, you can take my word for that."

Nobody doubted it. The writers who traveled with the ball club and knew most of what went on behind the scenes were aware that Mickey would have married Merlyn Johnson already if the front office hadn't told him they would be a lot happier if he waited until the season was over. Mickey agreed to wait, and Merlyn agreed to wait for him, but a young man of nineteen is never certain that his girl won't see somebody she likes better if he lets her run around without a wedding ring on her finger, and that was the way it was with Mickey. It didn't do his hitting any good. As a matter of fact for a while he did less hitting in Kansas City than he had been doing in New York. When he left the Yankees, Mickey's batting average was .260. He had made 64 hits, batted in 45 runs, and had hit 7 home runs, 5 triples and 9 doubles. After a single in his first game with the Blues, he failed to get a hit in his next 18 times at bat. When his father drove up from Commerce to spend a few days with him in Kansas City, he talked about quitting the game. It's hard now to believe that he could have meant it because he had already seen enough of what the game could mean to him to realize what he would be giving up, but he was a discouraged kid and it's human nature for a boy in a spot like that to give in to a little crying on his father's shoulder. That's what fathers are for. But fathers are also for stiffening a son's spine when it needs stiffening, and that's what Mutt Mantle did. "Maybe it's come too easy for you, Mickey," he said bluntly. "But it isn't always going to be easy and you've got to learn how to take it. It doesn't do any good to sit around feeling sorry for yourself. You've got to have the guts to get out there and do something about it. If you don't think you can, then come on back home with me and I'll get you a job in the mines."

Nobody ever could get through to Mickey the way his father

could. By the time Elven Mantle went back to Commerce, Mickey was on his way back up to .300. On August 24, after 40 games with Kansas City in which he had hit .364, with 11 home runs and an even 50 runs batted in, Mickey was recalled by the Yankees. He joined the club for a series in Cleveland and Stengel put him at number two in the batting order, behind Phil Rizzuto. Mickey made his return to the big leagues a hopeful occasion by coming up with one hit in four times at bat. The next day, swinging against the wide-breaking curve balls of big Mike Garcia, Mickey really celebrated the change of uniform. He drove in two runs with a homer and a double, and after that he was on his way. In the 37 games he played for the Yankees at the tag end of the season he hit a solid .283, good enough to convince Stengel that the kid belonged in the World Series lineup against the Giants, who had perpetrated "The Little Miracle of Coogan's Bluff" on the wings of Bobby Thomson's home run.

It was a short Series for Mickey. He didn't get a hit in the first game, and in the second, which he began in the unaccustomed role of lead-off man by dragging a bunt single past the pitcher's mound, he scared the daylights out of himself, his father, who was in the stands, and about 60,000 other people by collapsing on the field in the fifth inning. Willie Mays was the Giant batter and Willie lined the ball sharply into deep right-center field. Mickey made for it and was almost there when he stumbled and fell flat on his face in the grass. DiMaggio, coming over to back up the play, grabbed the ball in time to make the out, then bent over Mickey's motionless body. "What's the matter, kid?" he called to him. But Mickey was out cold and DiMaggio shouted in to the Yankee bench for a stretcher. It was discovered later that he had tripped over the wooden cover of a drainage outlet in the outfield and had badly wrenched his knee and had lost consciousness from the shock and the pain. The Yankees were vastly relieved to know that all he needed was treatment and rest.

Mickey went home a week later with the comforting knowledge

that the Commissioner's Office would, in a few weeks, mail him a check for $6,446.09 as his share of the winning team's loot from the Series. The extra money didn't exactly cast a pall over his marriage to Merlyn two days before Christmas in Merlyn's home town. Mickey had reached his twentieth birthday in October; Merlyn was nineteen. The kid was a married man now, an established major-leaguer, a rookie no longer. Pretty soon, with shocking unexpectedness, he was going to have to take the last long step into manhood and assume the burden of breadwinner for his mother, his three brothers (the twins, Ray and Roy, and a younger boy, Larry) and his sister, Barbara.

Elven Mantle had not been well for some time. Going to New York for the Series had been a strain on him, but somebody would have had to chain him down to keep him from going. Back home, he tried to convince himself that he would be all right in a few weeks, that all he needed to do was rest up and get his strength back, but before long he had to take a leave of absence from his job. He simply couldn't report in any more. Mickey knew all this, but nobody had prepared him for the seriousness of his father's condition, and he was stunned when they told him in New York, the first week of May, 1953, that Mutt Mantle was dead of cancer in a Denver hospital. He went home to help his family bury his father, the man who more than anyone else in the world had put him into a Yankee uniform, and he came back to do a man's work. He has done it ever since, in good health and bad, playing with his legs hurting more often than not, but always running like Ty Cobb and hitting like Babe Ruth and electrifying the crowds as few ballplayers have in the long history of the game.

If you want to pinpoint the time when Mickey left behind his apprenticeship (and regardless of the miraculously high level on which it was pitched, it was still an apprenticeship) and assumed the place everyone had known all along he was intended to occupy as one of the acknowledged superstars of the game, you would have

to look at the season of 1956. That was the summer of Mickey
Mantle's coming to greatness. He still had to contend with an astonishing assortment of physical handicaps, as he would always have to
do as long as he played baseball, but he brushed them off and swept
through the American League like an Oklahoma twister. He created
just as much havoc, too. Even the usually terse annual report of the
Official American League Batting Records, distributed by the Howe
News Bureau of Chicago, permitted itself the rare observation that,
"A summation of the American League batting figures for the 1956
season may well be entitled the Mickey Mantle Story." Mickey led
the league in batting with a .353 average, eight points in front of
Ted Williams; he hit 52 home runs, more than any Yankee except
Babe Ruth had ever hit and more than had ever been hit up to that
point by any player in the history of the American League except
Ruth, Hank Greenberg and Jimmy Foxx; and he batted in 130
runs, also a league-leading figure. Just for extras, he scored the most
runs, 132, and hit for the most total bases, 376. "It is cause for
rejoicing on the part of the Yankees," said *Sport* magazine in
presenting Mickey its award as Man of the Year in sport, "that
Mickey Mantle has reached this stage at the age of twenty-five. He
will be the man of many another year before he is through."

There was a big luncheon at Toots Shor's for Mickey in connection with the magazine's award and practically everybody who was
anybody in New York baseball circles turned out for the occasion,
including the Dodgers' two Walters, O'Malley and Alston, who
agreed that they had seen enough of Mickey to know he fully
deserved the award—in fact, they had seen enough of him, period.
Phil Rizzuto, just getting ready to move into the broadcasting
booth at the Stadium, was there, along with Yogi Berra and Whitey
Ford and Billy Martin, and Phil had some interesting things to say
about Mickey. "Lots of times I would look around behind me on the
field when things were in doubt, and I'd see Mickey out there in
center field, and I'd feel better right away. I only felt that way

about one other player, and that was Joe DiMaggio. It's a feeling only a player like that can give you, that there's somebody out there who can pull a tough game out for you, who can turn the game around all by himself. Mickey is just like Joe in that respect. In fact, the only difference, I'd say, between Mickey and Joe is that when Mickey struck out, he would say some things that Joe would never say."

A lot of jokes were made about the report that Mickey was supposed to sign a new contract while he was in town and that the Yankees had better lock up all the vaults at 745 Fifth Avenue. Dan Daniel of the *World-Telegram* was particularly funny about it. "I'm not up here to geld the lily," he said—"that's right, *geld*—but I'm not averse to boosting the price a little when Mickey goes in to talk with George Weiss, Lee MacPhail, Roy Hamey, Dan Topping and the whole corps of salary depressers. Because when it comes to Mantle in a baseball talent sense, there ain't no second. . . . I was in Phoenix when he showed up in 1951, and the way he hit that baseball I remember picking a ball up one day just to examine it and make sure it wasn't a trick. But it wasn't any Goldsmith 90 Rocket. It was an official American League baseball, the same one he's been hitting ever since. . . . Gentlemen, Mickey Mantle is number one and the rest of the field ain't nowhere."

The chances are Mickey most enjoyed listening to Dan Topping, the man who, with Del Webb, owns the Yankees. "I can see I made a mistake coming up here last night from Florida," Topping said. "I thought Mickey had already signed. But no matter. When he gets this award Mickey is getting everything he deserves, and he's going to get everything he deserves from the Yankees, too. Thank God, I'm not going to sit with MacPhail and Weiss when he gets it. But you go in there and get it, Mickey. You deserve it."

That was like handing Mickey the key to the Yankees' bank account, but Topping knew what he was doing. The Yankees were glad to pay him the $75,000 he signed for the next day, they were glad to pay him the $80,000 they raised him to a couple of years later, and even happier to pay him the $100,000 he signed for in 1962 and 1963. Baseball had had only two other $100,000 ball-players before Mickey, Joe DiMaggio and Stan Musial. He was in good company and he belonged there, not just because of the money he was being paid but because of the talent and the desire and the guts that earned the money.

Nobody can guess how many home runs will stand to Mickey Mantle's credit when he reaches the end of his career. In Mantle's case you can't figure so many per year and so many years left, because you never know if Mickey is going to play a full season or half a season and you never know which season might turn out to be his last. Mickey doesn't know, either, and that's the key to his personality and his approach to life as well as to baseball. He never forgets that his father died in his forties. He will never allow himself to forget that his own osteomyelitis, although controlled, apparently cannot be cured. He knows with grim certainty that there are diseases even the miracles of modern medicine cannot cure. It isn't so much that he is afraid he, too, is destined for a short life and a merry one as that he refuses to count on anything. All he knows is that it's up to him to make the most of what he has while he has it. That's why he's such a perfectionist; that's why he gets so angry at himself when he strikes out.

Milton Gross of the New York *Post* sat with Mickey and his mother in her Commerce house some years ago and heard her tell him, "Even when you were a little bitty thing you were never satisfied. When you were playing in the Pee Wee League and you got a single, you wanted a double. When you pitched in high school and you struck out fifteen, you wanted to strike out sixteen. It's still the same way now."

"Ma," Mickey said quietly, "now I got to ask you something. That was the way Pa wanted it, wasn't it?"

Lovell Mantle bent over her knitting. "Yes," she said, nodding her head, "that was the way he wanted it."

"Then that's the way I want it," Mickey said.

Chapter 9

Just hold them for a few innings, fellas. I'll
think of something.—CHARLIE DRESSEN

IN the spring of 1956, the year Tommy Henrich was
one of their coaches under Bill Rigney, the Giants threw a cocktail
party for the newspapermen covering the ball club at a fancy restaurant in Phoenix called the Green Lantern, where the parking lot
attendants ride on horses and wear suits of armor. Sometime during
the evening there was a little group sitting in a corner of the room
listening to Henrich and Bucky Walters, the fine National League
pitcher who had managed the Cincinnati Reds for a couple of seasons, talk baseball. The subject was how much a manager means to
a ball club. "The main thing he can do," Bucky was saying, "is get
the most out of his ballplayers." "What about strategy?" somebody
in the group asked. Henrich fielded the question: "I don't think
there's much difference between managers as far as strategy is concerned. I've always believed that everybody who wears a major-
league uniform, except maybe the very young kids and the few real
knotheads, knows just about everything there is to know about
baseball tactics. The game really isn't quite as complicated as some
people like to let on, you know." Bucky nodded in agreement and

grinned. "That's a fact," he said. "Hell, if the game was half as complicated as some of these writers make out it is, a lot of us boys from the farm would never have been able to make a living at it."

It's one of baseball's oldest and most durable arguments, whether or not a good manager actually can win ball games for his team, can, for instance, make the difference between finishing first and finishing second or third. Henrich and Walters weren't saying he couldn't, they simply were saying that his main contribution was made not in the area of tactics but in handling his men properly and getting out of them everything they had to give. The chances are most baseball men lean toward this viewpoint. Not many think any one manager knows more about how the game should be played than the other managers do, but all of them are convinced that a strong man in the dugout can help his ball club win a lot of games it might otherwise lose. The good manager puts his stamp on a team just as a good editor puts his stamp on his magazine or a good company president puts his stamp on his organization. He lays down the rules and he enforces them; he sets the pace and he determines the goal. His personality becomes the ball club's personality and his character the ball club's character.

No manager ever meant more to a ball club than Joe McCarthy meant to the Yankees he managed from 1931 to 1946. Joe had never played a game in the major leagues but he had learned his trade well in the minors. By the time he won his first pennant with the Louisville Colonels of the Southern Association in 1921 he was regarded in baseball as one of the finest managers in the minor leagues. He was known as a strict disciplinarian but at the same time an understanding man who could encourage the player who needed help as effectively as he could clamp down on the wise guy, the loafer or the playboy. Frank Graham, in his fine book *The New York Yankees,* tells what Earle Combs, one of the finest of Yankee outfielders and a player developed by McCarthy at Louisville, had to say about Joe's patience and kindliness.

"The first day he put me in center field," Earle said, "I was so nervous I could hardly see straight. I muffed the first ball that was hit to me. Joe never said a word to me when I went in to the bench at the end of the inning, and he didn't say anything a couple of innings later when I played a single into a triple. Finally, in the eighth inning, with the score tied and a couple of men on base, somebody hit a single out to center and I swore to myself as I ran in to pick up the ball that I would catch it and hold it if it killed me. Well, I didn't, and for a while I wished it had killed me. The ball went right through my legs and rolled all the way to the fence. I made up my mind right there that as soon as I got into the clubhouse and got dressed I was going to quit baseball for good. McCarthy wasn't going to get a chance to fire me. I would quit first. . . . When we got to the clubhouse, I guess McCarthy could tell how I felt by the way I looked. He came over to me and said, 'Forget it. You're still my center fielder.' Then he laughed and patted me on the shoulder. 'Listen,' he said, 'if I can stand it, I guess you can.' You know, I think I can say that from that minute on I was a professional ballplayer."

When William Wrigley, Jr., was looking for a manager for his Chicago Cubs before the 1926 season, some of his advisers told him about McCarthy. "He's a major-league manager in a minor-league town," they said, and urged him to give McCarthy the job. Wrigley did, and in his third season with the Cubs, McCarthy paid back the chewing-gum man with a National League pennant. He lost the World Series to the Athletics, though, and late in the 1930 season he lost his job to the man he had asked general manager William C. Veeck (father of Bill) to obtain for him in 1939 as his second baseman, the former player-manager of the Cardinals, Rogers Hornsby. A lot of his friends had warned Joe not to take on Hornsby, that Rog would surely try to steal his job from him, but Joe had said, "I'll take a chance on him. He can hit and he can play second base. I'm not afraid of him."

Even including the way he finally lost his job, Joe learned some priceless lessons during his hitch with the Cubs. The first one—and one he never forgot—was his trouble with Grover Cleveland Alexander. One of the game's great pitchers, Old Pete, as everybody called him, liked to take a drink when the spirit moved him, and the spirit moved him often and he seldom stopped at one. Once an automatic 20-game winner, he had managed to win fifteen games for the Cubs in 1925 and was still a valuable pitcher, but McCarthy knew he had no chance of enforcing his ideas of discipline on the rest of the ballplayers if he allowed Alexander to do as he pleased. He tried hard to get Pete to go on the wagon for the duration of the season, and when that didn't work he tried even harder to make sure that the old-timer at least showed up at the ball park every day in shape to work. It was no use. Alexander, who had been in and out of sanitariums "taking the cure" ever since he came home from World War I, and who was soon to lose his beloved wife Aimee because of his inability to control his drinking, was too far gone to change now. Finally, late in June, McCarthy fired him. Hornsby took him on in St. Louis, and, as every schoolboy knows, Old Pete provided a glorious bit of relief pitching in the climatic moments of the World Series that fall, striking out Tony Lazzeri with the bases loaded to help the Cardinals beat the Yankees. He won nine games for the Cardinals during the regular season, and McCarthy could have used those nine games, but with Alexander gone he was able to shape his ball club in his own image and not Old Pete's, and that was more important than nine victories.

Joe was more successful with Hack Wilson, then a slugging rookie up from Toledo of the American Association. Hack liked to go out on the town, too, but he showed up at the ball park on time every day and worked his head off, and McCarthy was determined that this was one battle he wasn't going to lose. It wasn't easy. Once, Wilson got a belly laugh out of the ballplayers at Joe's expense when Joe put a couple of worms in a glass of alcohol and showed how the alcohol killed them and asked Hack if he saw any lesson in that. Hack said, "Sure. If I keep on drinkin' likker I'll never have no worms." But in the end McCarthy's patience prevailed. Hack Wilson never became an advertisement for the Woman's Christian Temperance Union but he became a fine ballplayer for the Chicago Cubs. He was a .321 hitter in McCarthy's first year as manager and a .356 hitter in McCarthy's last year. Different people, Joe was learning, respond to different handling.

McCarthy might have stayed in Chicago a long time if he hadn't had such a humiliating experience in the 1929 World Series. Not only did the Cubs lose every game but one, but the way they lost the fourth game left Joe vulnerable to every wisecracking, second-guessing sportswriter in town. Trailing in the Series two games to one, the Cubs seemed certain to tie it up when they took an 8–0 lead into the last half of the seventh inning at Shibe Park in Philadelphia. Even when the first man up for the A's in that inning, Al Simmons, hit the ball into the seats for a home run, the only thing anybody thought it meant was that the Cubs' pitcher, Charley Root, had lost his shutout. But then Jimmy Foxx singled, Bing Miller singled and Jimmy Dykes singled, and it was 8–2 with runners on first and third. When Joe Boley came through with a single to score Miller, it was 8–3, with nobody out, and the sellout crowd began to sit up and take notice. Connie Mack sent in George Burns to pinch-hit and he raised a pop fly to shortstop Woody English for the first out. But then Max Bishop singled home Jimmy Dykes to make the score 8–4, and McCarthy decided it was time to put in a new pitcher. He brought in Art Nehf, a southpaw, hoping to choke off the next two hitters, Mule Haas and Mickey Cochrane, both left-handed. But Haas whacked a fly ball to deep center field that Hack Wilson lost in the sun, and by the time he recovered it the score was 8–7, and where had that beautiful lead gone? Cochrane walked and McCarthy replaced Nehf with Sheriff Blake. The Sheriff was clipped for successive singles by Simmons and Foxx, the two fel-

lows who had started the whole thing, and the park was in an up-
roar as Cochrane scored the tying run on Foxx's hit. Desperate,
McCarthy called for Pat Malone, the relief specialist who occupies
an immortal niche in baseball literature for his statement, "I owe it
all to clean living and a fast outfield." Pat proceeded to load up the
bases once again by hitting Bing Miller with a pitched ball, and then
he settled down to pitch to Jimmy Dykes. Dykes hit a looping fly ball
to left field and the Philadelphia fans whooped as they saw that
Simmons surely would be able to score after the catch. Then their
excitement turned to hysteria as Riggs Stephenson, playing left
field for the Cubs, failed to catch up to the ball at all. It fell safely
to the ground as both Simmons and Foxx raced across the plate with
the runs that put the A's ahead, 10–8, which is the way the game
ended two innings later. It was a mortifying defeat, and McCarthy's
Chicago critics never let him live it down. They blamed the
pitchers, they blamed Hack Wilson for losing that fly ball in the
sun, and they blamed Stephenson for messing up the ball Dykes hit,
but they blamed McCarthy for everything. If it was true, as Mc-
Carthy always thought, that Hornsby was working behind his back
to succeed him, he had given him all the ammunition he needed.

But the release Wrigley and Veeck gave him was a blessing in dis-
guise for Joe because it set him at liberty at the precise moment the
Yankees were looking for a manager to take over from Bob Shawkey. Ed Barrow, the Yankees' general manager, asked Joe to come
up from Philadelphia, where he was watching the World Series between the Athletics and the Cardinals, for a talk with him and
Colonel Ruppert at Ruppert's Fifth Avenue apartment. After a
long, candid discussion of what the Yankees expected of their manager, Ruppert smilingly approved as Barrow and McCarthy shook
hands on contract terms.

Joe was so nervous when he was introduced after the Series to the
press in New York as the Yankees' new manager that, when somebody asked him to say a few words into a microphone, he stammered

and said, "Colonel Huston, I—" then blushed furiously as he realized that he had used the name of the wrong colonel, the one who had left the Yankees in 1923. Ruppert laughed along with everybody else and said gently, "Maybe McCarthy will be around here long enough so he will get to know me better." As matters turned out, Joe stayed around for fifteen years, long enough to win eight pennants and seven world championships for the patrician brewer who told him, that first night in his luxurious apartment, "I warn you, McCarthy, I don't like to finish second."

McCarthy wasted no time making it clear to the Yankees who reported to him at St. Petersburg in the spring that he was the boss. Never, in his long association with the club, did he compromise the first principle he brought with him from Chicago: he and he alone was running the ball club. Frank Graham remembers that the first day Joe walked into the clubhouse at Yankee Stadium he noticed a card table in a corner of the room. "What's that for?" he asked Fred Logan, the clubhouse man. "That's the players' card table," Logan said, puzzled. "Take it out of here," McCarthy ordered coldly as the ballplayers stood around the room and listened. "This is a clubhouse, not a clubroom," the manager said. "When you come in here, put your minds on baseball."

McCarthy had few complaints about his players in 1931 but the Yankees didn't win. It was a lineup studded with names to remember—Babe Ruth, Lou Gehrig, Tony Lazzeri, Earle Combs, Bill Dickey, Ben Chapman, Lyn Lary, Red Ruffing, Lefty Gomez, Herb Pennock. Ruth hit 49 home runs, Gehrig hit 46, Chapman stole 61 bases, and Gomez won 21 ball games, but the Yankees didn't have quite enough moxie to push the Athletics off the top of the hill. They finished where Colonel Ruppert had told McCarthy he didn't like to finish, second.

It was different in '32. Joe was sitting firmly in the saddle. He was a perfectionist, a hard-driving wagonmaster, a fighter. He was proud of the Yankee uniform he wore, proud of the Ruths and

Gehrigs and Lazzeris who wore it with him, and he didn't want anybody around him who didn't share his pride. McCarthy's years in the bushes had taught him to be patient with the mechanical mistakes of ballplayers but he had no tolerance for weaknesses of character. Clubhouse lawyers, prima donnas, rowdies, malcontents and drinkers were cleaned out as fast as he spotted them. It meant a lot to Joe to be in Yankee Stadium and he didn't want a ballplayer on his roster who didn't feel the same way. In 1932 he and his men, from Babe Ruth to substitute catcher Arndt Jorgens, saw eye to eye on what had to be done and how to do it, and they won 107 ball games to take the pennant hands down.

The Chicago Cubs won the championship of the National League, and the Cubs were the team McCarthy would have chosen if he had been allowed to pick his World Series opponent. Even though Charley Grimm, and not Hornsby, was managing them now, they were still the same Cubs who had fired him, and he was eager to get even with them. The Yankee ballplayers knew how he felt about it, and anyway, they had their own grievance against the Cubs. One of their old teammates, Mark Koenig, called up from the Pacific Coast League in August by Grimm, after he took over the club from Hornsby, had played good baseball for Chicago down the homestretch but had been voted only a quarter of a share of the World Series money. The Yankees were savagely scornful of such "cheap" tactics and minced no words in letting the Cubs know how they felt.

Babe Ruth started it. He sat in the Yankees' dugout and watched the Cubs come out on the field for the opening game of the series in New York. When he spotted Koenig he boomed out in his inimitable, hoarse voice, "Hey, Mark, who are those cheap skates with you?" Probably Koenig was more embarrassed than his grim-faced teammates, but the other Yankees joined Ruth in a no-letup barrage of the roughest jockeying ever aimed at any big-league ball club. "Nickel nursers" was about the mildest epithet shouted at the

Cubs by the derisive Yankees. Then, by way of making sure that their name-calling didn't boomerang, and mindful of McCarthy's grudge against the Chicago front office as well as their own in behalf of Koenig, the Yankees buried the stunned Cubs in four straight games. The game best remembered through the years is the third, the one in which Ruth brazenly "called his shot" against Charley Root and followed through with a prodigious home run to the deepest point of the center-field bleachers, exactly where his princely wave had indicated he would hit it.

Joe McCarthy and the Yankees were sitting on top of the world after that. But many of McCarthy's best ballplayers, beginning with the incomparable Ruth, were getting old. Ruth slipped to .301 in 1933 and to .288, a puny batting average for the great man, in 1934. The Yankees gave him his release in 1935 after he had waged his last campaign to persuade Colonel Ruppert to give him the managership.

McCarthy remained manager of the Yankees as long as Colonel Ruppert lived and until Joe made up his own mind that he had put in a full hitch and it was time for a change. The pennants piled up —1936, with the young slugger from San Francisco, Joe DiMaggio, coming on to take up some of the slack left by the departure of Ruth, 1937, 1938, 1939, 1941, 1942, 1943. Eight pennants and seven world championships in a span of not quite fifteen seasons. Jimmy Dykes might call him a "push-button manager" in left-handed tribute to the remarkable efficiency of the Yankee organization, but Ed Barrow knew what he was talking about when he looked out from behind those bushy eyebrows of his and said, "Never underestimate McCarthy. He was a truly great manager. He was the finest handler of young players I've ever seen." No one who knows the Yankee story intimately would deny that even after he left the club in August, 1945, wiring in his resignation to a man he neither liked nor respected, Larry MacPhail, the McCarthy impress remained on the Yankees for a long time.

In a similar way, the popular image of the modern Dodgers, as

opposed to the old three-men-sliding-into-one-base Dodgers of
Babe Herman and Frenchy Bordagaray and Van Lingle Mungo, was
largely the design of one strong-willed manager, Leo Durocher.
Wills just don't come any stronger than Durocher's. Ever since his
kid days, when he was the best pool player for his age and weight
in West Springfield, Massachusetts, Leo has been battling and
scheming to win. First as a ballplayer, then as a manager. He has
made more newspaper copy than any other manager of our time,
with the single exception of Casey Stengel, because the public sees
in him the fearless warrior every man would like to believe himself
to be. His appeal, and his basic strength as a manager, is the primitive admiration we all have for the consummate fighter, the man
who isn't afraid to stick his neck out, to risk the whole bankroll on
one roll of the dice, who swaggers down the street like John L.
Sullivan with a chip on his shoulder, defying everybody including
the cop on the beat to knock it off.

Combative is the word for Leo. "I'm fighting out there every
day," he raged at his Dodgers one day in an angry clubhouse scene
during his first year as manager, "because I love the big leagues. I
love this life, I love these good hotels, I love these good restaurants,
I love this good dough. What's the matter with you guys? You
want to go back to the tank towns, the blue-plate specials, the
overnight buses and two hundred and fifty bucks a month?"

That's the way Durocher has always played it. If he has had
luck along the way it's because he has made his own luck. His
mother had a point when she was asked, back in 1928, what she
thought of Leo's making the World Series as a utility infielder for
the Yankees. "I tell you, mister," Mrs. Durocher said philosophi-
cally, "if my Leo fell in the Connecticut River, he wouldn't get wet."
The truth is that Leo has the kind of luck you occasionally see in
the gambler who is both skillful and bold. There is a good deal more
to Durocher the manager than the heart of a lion and the tongue of
a fishwife. He is a smart cookie, insensitive to danger, the possessor
of a hard-bitten, school-of-hard-knocks shrewdness which weighs

alternatives in lightning-fast calculations and almost intuitively comes up with the right one. Leo spices his tactics, which are basically sound, with the tabasco of imagination—he's an incurable hunch player—and he has stolen a lot of ball games that more conservative managers thought they had safely in the bag.

Leo doesn't particularly care what happens to the people who get in his way while he roars hell-bent down the track. He doesn't go out of his way looking for people to hurt but if somebody happens to get caught in the switches Leo figures that's strictly his problem. "Why don't you try being a nice guy for a change?" Red Barber needled him good-naturedly one day when Leo's Dodgers were at the Polo Grounds for a game with Mel Ott's Giants, and Leo was putting the rap on a few National League ballplayers while he held court for the press before the game. "A nice guy?" Aroused, Leo pointed across the field to the Giants' dugout. "Look over there! Do you know a nicer guy than Mel Ott? He's the nicest guy in the world, and where is he? In last place. I'm *not* a nice guy and I'm in first place. Take it from me, nice guys finish last!"

It was the ruthless side of Durocher that showed in the way he handled Pete Reiser when Pistol Pete was the hottest young ballplayer in the National League and seemed to be headed for one of the game's great careers if he could just figure out a way to stop banging his head into the outfield wall chasing fly balls. "In two and a half years in the minors, three seasons of army ball and ten years in the majors, Pete Reiser was carried off the field eleven times," Bill Heinz said in a story he wrote about Pete a few years ago. "Nine times he regained consciousness either in the clubhouse or in hospitals. He broke a bone in his right elbow, throwing. He broke both ankles, tore a cartilage in his left knee, and ripped the muscles in his left leg, sliding. Seven times he crashed into outfield walls, dislocating his left shoulder, breaking his right collarbone, and five times ending up in an unconscious heap on the ground. Twice he was beaned."

Nobody knows the heights Reiser might have reached if he had remained whole. When he was young, and healthy, he was as fine a center fielder as there ever was, as good as the young DiMaggio, as good as the young Willie Mays, as good as the young Mickey Mantle. He could do it all, run, hit, and throw. He not only was willing to run through a wall to catch a fly ball and save a ball game, he tried to do it again and again. He left his genius splattered against those walls. In 1941, his first full season with the Dodgers, they couldn't get him out, and with his .343 average he became the first rookie ever to win the National League batting championship. Then, in the middle of the 1942 season, he caromed off the wall in St. Louis trying to catch a long drive by Enos Slaughter. "Actually, I did catch the ball," Pete remembers, "but then I couldn't stop and I ran into the wall and dropped it. I was able to pick it up and throw it to Pee Wee, but then when I tried to take a step, everything blacked out. I woke up the next morning in the hospital."

Doc Hyland, the famous St. Louis "baseball doctor," told Pete he didn't think he should play any more baseball that season. His head might not be able to stand it. But after a couple of days in the hospital Pete put on his clothes and went out on the street and took a cab to the railroad station. He rode the train to Pittsburgh, where the Dodgers had gone, and got there around dinnertime. There was a night game on, so he went right out to Forbes Field and walked into the clubhouse. Durocher took one look at him, grinned happily and said, "Put on the suit, Pete." Reiser had enough sense to say no, he'd better not. "Not tonight, skipper," he said. "I wouldn't be any good to you, anyway. I just wanted to watch." But Leo was persistent. "Come on," he insisted. "I wouldn't let you play. But it'll scare these guys just to see you sitting on the bench suited up." So Pete put on his working clothes and sat down in the dugout.

The game was in the fourteenth inning, and the Dodgers had

runners on first and second, when Durocher started stalking up and down looking for a pinch hitter. He had used up everybody except the pitchers. "I'll hit," Pete said, and got up and took a bat out of the rack. Leo looked hard at him. "Okay," he said, "okay. Just a single, Pete, that's all we need. You won't even have to run hard." So Reiser walked up there and dug in and hit a line shot over the third baseman's head that rolled all the way to the wall in the left-field corner. Pete started running, and he seemed to be running as fast as ever, but when he rounded first he fell flat on his face and just lay there. When he woke up again he was back in the hospital, in Pittsburgh this time. He was seeing a lot of hospitals. Durocher was in the room, looking happy that Pete was waking up. "We won it, Pete," Leo said. "How do you feel?" Pete made a face. "How do you think I feel?" he said. Leo put a hand on his shoulder. "Pete," he said in that compelling voice of his that makes you think he's emptying all of his pockets just for you, "you're better with one leg and one eye than anybody else I've got." "Yeah," Pete said, "and that's the way I'll end up, with one leg and one eye."

It would be a mistake to conclude that Leo didn't care what happened to Reiser. He cared very much, because Pistol Pete could win ball games for him, but Durocher simply cannot resist throwing in all of his marbles to win today. One of Leo's enduring baseball maxims is the one about using the best pitcher you have today. "You don't save a pitcher for tomorrow," Leo says. "Tomorrow it may rain." That's Durocher in a nutshell. It was the same do-or-die attitude that cost him his job with the Yankees. Leo hit Ed Barrow for a raise at the end of the 1929 season, even though his batting average had dropped from the .270 he had managed in 1928 to an un-Yankee .246 in '29. Barrow thought he was a fresh kid and said so, but the raise he offered struck Leo as more of an insult than the estimate of his behavior. Leo shrugged and started to walk out of the office. "If you go out that door," Barrow said sternly, and there never was a general manager who could be sterner, "you're going right out of the American League." Leo never even looked back, and in a short time he was picked up on waivers by the Cincinnati Reds, who moved him along a few seasons later to the St. Louis Cardinals.

It was probably all for the best. Baseball would have been infinitely poorer if the Cardinals and later the Dodgers had missed Durocher. Leo always has contended that the National is a more rough-and-ready league than the American, and it was Leo who hung the nickname "Gas House Gang" on that raffish crew managed by Frank Frisch in the glory days of Dizzy Dean, Ducky Medwick, Kayo Delancey and Rip Collins. Frank Graham was sitting on the Cardinals' bench when the club came to New York for a series with the Giants and he talked for a while with Dizzy Dean and Durocher. Dean, arguing that the National League was tougher, offered the observation that if the Cardinals were transferred into the American League then and there, and given the terrible handicap of the won-lost percentage owned by the lowly St. Louis Browns, they could still win the pennant. "Aah," Durocher said scornfully, "they wouldn't let a Gas House ball club like this one play in that nice clean league."

Leo made his reputation with that Gas House ball club. He drove Frisch half crazy, but then so did Dean and Medwick and the rest. Leo had found a home; he fitted into the Cardinals' clubhouse like part of the furniture. He and the rest of that colorful gang spoke the same language, much of it unprintable. They heaped abuse on the opposition with a rich stream of profanity and followed it up by playing ball just as excitingly as they said they could. No shrinking violets, they welcomed Leo as one of their own the first day they laid eyes on him. He might have stayed with the Cardinals longer if he had been able to restrain himself in his raging arguments with Frisch, but that was too much to ask and eventually the Dutchman stormed into the front office and told Branch Rickey, the boss, "it's got to be either him or me." So Rickey, unwilling to lose a successful manager, peddled Durocher to the struggling Brooklyn Dodgers for four used-up ballplayers, Joe Stripp, Roy Henshaw, Johnny Cooney and Jim Bucher. In a way Rickey hated to see the lippy Leo go, although he had gone on record as saying of him, "He has an amazingly fertile talent for making a difficult situation immediately worse." They were to see much more of each other in the years ahead.

Leo didn't take kindly to the trade and was still grumbling when he reported to Burleigh Grimes, the old spitballer who was managing the Dodgers, in the spring of 1938, but by World Series time he had been appointed manager and was all smiles. This was what he had really wanted; now he could spread his wings. Baseball has never had a more combustible combination in the front office and the dugout than Larry MacPhail, the president of the Dodgers, and Durocher. The fur flew between them almost constantly. But Durocher, fired so many times that he lost count, hung in there and came up with a pennant for MacPhail in 1941. MacPhail even fired him the night Leo brought the ball club home on the train with the pennant freshly won, but that was because Leo had told MacPhail he could get on the train at 125th Street in New York and instead the engineer took it all the way through to Grand Central Terminal, leaving MacPhail standing on the platform shrieking wild threats to the New York Central Railroad, the Brotherhood of Railroad Engineers, traveling secretary Harold Parrott and especially Leo Durocher.

Leo suffered agonies of torture when the Yankees swept through his carefully patched together Dodger team in five games in the World Series. With Dolph Camilli on first, Billy Herman, the old Chicago Cub, on second, rookie Peewee Reese at short and Cookie Lavagetto on third, Ducky Medwick, Pete Reiser and veteran Dixie Walker in the outfield, Mickey Owen to do the catching and Freddie Fitzsimmons, Curt Davis, Whit Wyatt, Larry French, Hugh Casey and Kirby Higbe to pitch, Leo thought he had a club that could give the Yankees a fight. The saddest day of all, for him, came on Sunday, October 5, in the fourth game. The Yankees had won two games and the Dodgers one as they squared off again at Ebbets Field. When the Yankees came to bat in the top of the ninth, the Dodgers led, 4–3, largely because of a booming home run by Pete Reiser. Hugh Casey was pitching in relief of Johnny Allen, and it looked as though it was all over but the shouting when Johnny Sturm grounded out to second and Casey himself threw out Red Rolfe. Then came one of those wildly unpredictable moments that make baseball what it is. Casey went to three and two on Tommy Henrich, then threw a breaking pitch that Henrich missed by a mile for what should have been the third strike and the end of the game. But Mickey Owen couldn't hold on to the ball. It rolled through him to the grandstand and Henrich ran down to first ahead of Owen's desperate throw. Upset and angry, Casey gave up a single to DiMaggio and a double to Charlie Keller that scored both Henrich and DiMaggio, putting the Yankees ahead, 5–4. Bill Dickey walked, then Joe Gordon doubled deep to left field and the score was 7–4. Brooklyn never knew a blacker day.

Leo was to know one just as black when Commissioner Albert B. ("Happy") Chandler suspended him for the season of 1947 after an ugly name-calling fracas between Durocher and MacPhail, who had moved across the river to become head man of the Yankees, after a spring exhibition game between the two clubs in Havana. Burt Shotton won the pennant with Leo's club that season and repeated the stunt the year after he took over permanently from Leo in the middle of July, 1948, when Durocher made the unbelievable jump from Ebbets Field to the Polo Grounds and signed to manage the New York Giants. The old-line Giant fans couldn't have been more shocked if Durocher had been appointed commissioner in place of Chandler. In fact, they would have preferred it. Brought up to hate the Dodgers and everything connected with them, especially Durocher, they choked on the thought that their beloved Giants were now to be run by this foul-mouthed upstart. Leo Durocher in the shoes of John McGraw, Bill Terry and Mel Ott!—it was sacrilege.

They said worse things when Leo finished fifth with the Giants in 1948 and fifth again the next season. But that was when the dandy little manager dug in his spikes and showed what he could do under pressure. He convinced Horace Stoneham that the club needed a major shake-up, and he engineered a Stoneham trade of Sid Gordon, Willard Marshall, Buddy Kerr and Sam Webb to the Braves for Alvin Dark and Eddie Stanky. A lot of people thought he was crazy, that he had given away a lot of power in exchange for a little finesse in the field, and they got on his back vigorously when the Braves opened the 1950 season at the Polo Grounds by sweeping a three-game series from the "rebuilt" Giants. But Leo finished a strong third that year, and in 1951 he produced the miracle finish that forever will stand as a monument to his ability to drive and inspire and literally drag a ball club that last few feet over the line to win. Even his second Giant pennant in 1954, and the crushing four-game sweep of the Cleveland Indians in the Series, has to take a back seat to the breathless surge of 1951 when Leo's Giants won 36 of their last 43 ball games to snatch the pennant right out of the Dodgers' hands. If you ever hear somebody say that managers don't win pennants, tell them about Leo Durocher at the Polo Grounds in 1951.

Tell them, too, about Casey Stengel at Yankee Stadium in that memorable stretch of years from 1949 through 1960. Like Joe McCarthy before him, Casey had to contend with the knockers who said the Yankees could win with Bob Hope in the dugout, but in his more than fifty years in baseball Casey has been knocked by experts. He doesn't bruise easily. When Dan Topping and Del Webb introduced him to the New York baseball writers as the new manager of the Yankees a couple of weeks after the World Series of 1948, which the Yankees weren't in, he promised in deadly earnest, "I won't fail. I never had so many good ballplayers before." It was a strangely hostile press corps Casey faced that day, even though many of the reporters were old friends going all the way back to his playing days with the Dodgers and the Giants. The misgivings they felt had nothing to do with Casey himself; they stemmed from resentment of the firing of his predecessor, Bucky Harris, a great favorite of the newspapermen and winner of one world championship in his two seasons as manager of the club. The writers felt that Harris had been fired simply because he had been hired by Larry MacPhail, that anyone who could be called MacPhail's man was *persona non grata* to the new owners, Topping and Webb. It didn't make Casey's job any easier, and it was hard enough on its merits. He had taken charge of a ball club that appeared to have seen its best days, a club that probably looked better on paper with names like DiMaggio, Berra, Henrich, Stirnweiss, Lindell, Woodling and Rizzuto than it would look on the ball field.

"Casey is either going to have to be very good or very funny," the pro-Harris men wrote, taking care to get in the jab that the Yankees had hired Casey the clown, the good-time Charlie, to keep the fans from paying too much attention to the ball club while George Weiss and his aides in the front office rebuilt it. Casey's reputation, of course, was richly deserved. Wasn't this the man who, after he had been traded from the Dodgers to the Pirates, had responded to the jeers of the fans at Ebbets Field one day by raising his cap at home plate and releasing a sparrow which promptly flew swiftly into the grandstand, thus allowing Casey to become the first player in baseball history to give back as good as he got in the bird department? Casey was one of the better outfielders in the big leagues for a dozen seasons with the Dodgers, Pirates, Phillies, Giants and Braves; he was good enough to hit .368 for the Giants in 1922 and to win two games from the Yankees in the 1923 World Series with dramatic home runs, one of them an inside-the-park spectacular. But people still thought of him as a clown.

That inside-the-park home run probably did more to add to his

reputation as a character than to his reputation as a hitter, all because of a story the great Damon Runyon wrote about it, a piece
of whimsy that has become one of the classics of sportswriting.
Casey makes the story even funnier when he tells it by remembering
that this was the summer he was courting Edna Lawson, one of the
prettiest residents of Glendale, California. Edna had agreed to
marry Casey in the fall but her parents hadn't yet met him. "So,
naturally," Casey says in that gravelly voice of his, "they were
somewhat curious about me and they used to read about me in the
papers every chance they got, which wasn't as often as they or I or
Edna would have liked. But the day after we beat the Yankees in
the first game of that World Series they couldn't wait to read about
me and my inside-the-park home run. So they started reading this
story which Damon Runyon had made up about me and if you
would look it up you would see how it went." It went like this:

This is the way old Casey Stengel ran yesterday afternoon running his
home run home.
This is the way old Casey Stengel ran running his home run home to a
Giant victory by a score of 5 to 4 in the first game of the World Series
of 1923.
This is the way old Casey Stengel ran running his home run home when
two were out in the ninth and the score was tied and the ball still bounding
inside the Yankee yard.
This is the way—
His mouth wide open.
His warped old legs bending beneath him at every stride.
His arms flying back and forth like those of a man swimming the crawl
stroke.
His flanks heaving, his breath whistling, his head far back.
Yankee infielders, passed by old Casey Stengel as he was running his
home run home, say Casey was muttering to himself, adjuring himself to
greater speed as a jockey mutters to his horse in a race, saying: "Go on,
Casey, go on."
The warped old legs, twisted and bent by many a year of baseball cam-

paigning, just barely held out under old Casey Stengel until he reached the plate, running his home run home.

Then he collapsed.

Casey claims that Edna beamed proudly after her father read the story.

"Well, Pop," she said, "what do you think of my Casey now?"

"I think," Mr. Lawson said pessimistically, "you'll be lucky if he lives to make the wedding."

But Casey survived the season, the wedding, and many another season in the hot sun that always makes his gargoyle face look like the face of a sea captain or a range rider. He began his career as a manager with the Worcester, Massachusetts, club of the Eastern League in 1925. He also served as president of the club, a circumstance which made it possible for him to escape when he was offered a chance to manage the crack Toledo Mud Hens of the Triple-A American Association. Judge Emil Fuchs, who owned the Boston Braves as well as the Worcester club, refused to give him permission to make the move, so Casey simply sat down in his office at the ball park and dictated a letter addressed to himself:

"Manager Charles Dillon Stengel is hereby and as of this date dismissed as manager of the Worcester, Eastern League, baseball club. Signed, Charles Dillon Stengel, President."

Casey did well enough at Toledo to be hired as a coach for the Brooklyn Dodgers under manager Max Carey in 1932. Now Casey was back in the majors, wearing again the first major-league uniform he had ever worn. At the end of the 1933 season, he was offered Carey's job. Much as he wanted to manage a big-league club, Stengel had too strong a sense of personal loyalty for that. He refused to say yes until he was allowed to put in a long-distance telephone call to Carey at his home in Florida and had been assured by his old boss that he was out of the picture for good and would be happy to see Casey take the job. Casey did, for $15,000 a year, less money than Carey, whose contract still had a year to run, was being paid not to manage the club.

It is no secret to anyone that Casey's early turns as a big-league manager, in Brooklyn and later in Boston with the Braves, were not noticeably distinguished. He never had the players and that was all there was to it, although when he was struck by a hit-and-run driver on a Boston street during the summer of 1943 and had to retire from the dugout to a hospital room (in the maternity ward, at that), a particularly caustic Boston sportswriter nominated the unknown driver as "the man who has done the most for Boston baseball this year." The man's charge was irresponsible, if not downright vindictive. Casey always gave the job everything he had, and what he didn't know about baseball wasn't worth knowing. He cared about nothing but baseball, lived and slept baseball, and gave every man who ever hired him 150 cents' worth of effort and dedication for every dollar he was paid.

With Brooklyn, in three seasons, he finished sixth, seventh and fifth. He had a few good ballplayers, catcher Al Lopez, infielder Tony Cuccinello and pitcher Van Mungo, but most of his hired hands were baseball buffoons. Casey's own favorite story of those days is about the time Frenchy Bordagaray, his mustached infielder, managed to get himself picked off second base in a game with the Cubs even though he hadn't made a visible move to take a lead off the bag. Casey catapulted out of the coaching box and raged at the umpire, "Whataya mean, out? The sonofagun was standing right on the bag. He never left it." The umpire, with the cold disdain that only an umpire can affect, didn't even lend Casey an ear. He dismissed him out of hand, and Casey, steaming like a teakettle, had to wait until the inning was over to turn his anger on the hapless Bordagaray. "Frenchy," he said, trying to control his exasperation but not succeeding very well, "how come you let that umpire get away with that? You never even took a lead off the bag. How could you be out?" Bordagaray was red-faced, but he was honest. "Well, you see, Case," he said nervously, "I was sorta doin' a little tap dance out there on the bag, and, well, to tell you the truth, what happened was, the guy tagged me between taps."

About the only good thing that happened to Stengel in Brooklyn was the way he and his ragamuffin ball club got even with manager Bill Terry of the Giants for Terry's celebrated crack before the ball clubs left New York to open spring training for the 1934 season. Terry, feeling as fat and sassy as only the manager of the world champions can feel, was asked by Roscoe McGowen of the *New York Times* what he thought of Brooklyn's chances for the coming season. "Brooklyn?" Terry asked, puffing on his one-dollar cigar. "Is Brooklyn still in the league?" It was one of those cracks, like Jimmy Dykes' push-button manager gibe, that live on for a long time. It lived much too long for Terry's comfort. The Giants came up to their last two games of the regular season dead even with Frank Frisch's Cardinals. Their last two games were with the Dodgers. If they were to take it all, they would have to win both; to lose even one would put a serious crimp in their struggle to stay alive in the pennant race.

"Let's see if we're still in the league," Casey suggested to his ball-players as they walked out onto the Polo Grounds field for the first game, and there wasn't a man in Dodger uniform who doubted that the skipper would chop off his arm at the elbow if it would help make Terry eat his words. Van Mungo made that first game an easy one for the Dodgers, winning 5–1, and the next day the Brooklyns, egged on by thousands of their Faithful who had made the subway trip across town to throw Terry's taunt back in his teeth, made old Casey the happiest sixth-place manager in baseball by winning again. But without ballplayers to work with he was doomed in Brooklyn, and he always knew it. Even his remarkably resilient spirit sagged on occasion, like the day his boys blew a doubleheader in Wrigley Field and Casey walked into a downtown Chicago barbershop and instructed the barber, "A haircut and a shave, please, and be careful you don't cut my throat. I may want to do that myself later." His last contract with the Brooklyn club carried through 1937 but, to the surprise of practically nobody, the directors voted to pay him off at the end of the 1936 season. Like the man who was there before him, Max Carey, he was paid not to manage the ball club for a year—a piece of history that has often been dredged up by anti-Stengel writers who chose to regard it as a sound professional judgment of Casey's ability.

After his yearlong vacation Casey went back to work as manager of the Boston Braves. It was at least as trying an experience as his stint in Brooklyn. He finished fifth in 1938, seventh in each of the next four seasons, and sixth in 1943. It's doubtful that he was especially heartbroken when the ownership of the club changed hands after the 1943 season and his resignation, tendered on his own initiative because he thought the new owners ought to have the right to put in their own manager, was accepted with polite thanks. At least he got back the $43,000 of his own money that he had invested in the Braves to help shore up the club's tottering financial structure.

This time Casey didn't stay out of work long. He was hired to manage the Milwaukee Brewers of the American Association, the league in which he had done so well with Toledo. Casey was hired by the directors of the club who were unaware that their president and principal stockholder, young Bill Veeck, took a poor view indeed of Stengel's qualifications. Bill was in the Pacific with the Marines. When he heard what had happened, he dashed off a letter that must be about as savage an indictment of Casey as any on record:

Gentlemen, I learned an hour ago the identity of our new manager. I've waited an hour to write this, hoping to cool off. So far it hasn't been too successful. To say that I'm very disappointed is putting it mildly. I'd like to have a complete explanation of where Stengel came from. Who suggested him? Who hired him? For how much and for how long? I don't want anything to do with Stengel, nor do I want him to have anything to do with anything I have a voice *in*.

I will now proceed to elucidate the above:

First, Stengel has never managed a winner. In my humble opinion, he is a poor manager.

Second, he has been closely connected with Bob Quinn and the operation of the Boston Braves. This in itself is enough to damn him.

Third, I don't believe that Stengel is a good judge of ballplayers so can be of no value to us in amassing future clubs.

Fourth, from my observation, Stengel is mentally a second-division major-leaguer. That is, he is entirely satisfied with a mediocre ball club as long as Stengel and his alleged wit are appreciated.

Fifth, I have no confidence in his ability, and rather than be continuously worried, I'd rather dispose of the whole damn thing. . . .

Bill didn't give in even when Casey brought the Brewers home seven games in front of the field and Casey let the directors who had hired him off the hook by quitting at the end of the season. But Veeck, recovering from a service injury in a hospital at Corona, California, did write Casey a friendly letter congratulating him on the job he had done for the Brewers and asking him to come see him if he had a chance. Casey, not one to hold a grudge, did, and the two marathon talkers took to each other immediately. When Veeck tried to buy the New York Giants from the Stoneham family and their associates that winter, he let it be known that the man he wanted to put in as manager was Casey Stengel.

After that, for Casey, there was a year working for the Yankees in Kansas City, where he finished a poor seventh with what George Weiss thought was the poorest crop of Yankee farmhands in years, and then three happy seasons with the Oakland Oaks across the bay from San Francisco. Casey won the Pacific Coast League pennant in his third year with the Oaks, and it didn't shock any of baseball's better-informed people that he came up with the lucky number when the Yankees went looking for a new manager after they dismissed Bucky Harris at the end of the 1948 season. There had been talk about Joe DiMaggio, Tommy Henrich, Al Simmons, Bill McKechnie and Bill Terry, but it was Casey Stengel who got the job.

Some newspapermen thought it was surprising, and Weiss had a piece of plain talk for them: "I've always been on friendly terms with Casey and Del Webb knew him fairly well out on the Coast. But he didn't get this job through friendship. The Yankees represent an investment of millions of dollars. They don't hand out jobs like that because they like your company. Stengel got the job because the Yankees think he can produce for them."

Casey had an equally blunt opinion, aimed particularly at those critics who thought he was signing on as a sort of vaudeville act to hold the center of the stage during the rebuilding period. "Clowning around is all right," Casey said, his eyes piercing right through the men sitting in a circle around him, "when you have a second-division ball club. It helps create some interest when you're going bad and it gives the boys something to write about besides losing streaks and bad players. But you don't have to always leave them laughing when you're up there—and I mean to be up there."

A man with less determination never would have brought the 1949 Yankees home where Casey did, in first place. These were the Yankees, and that big fellow with the distinctive batting stance and the graceful way of camping under a fly ball was Joe DiMaggio, but you couldn't blame Stengel in the spring of his first year with the club if he felt that the whole thing was a mirage. DiMaggio's famous foot injury kept him out of the lineup for the first sixty-five games, and how would you like to be a manager with Stengel's record, suddenly inheriting a player like Joe DiMaggio, and finding out he couldn't play? His team piled up an incredible record of seventy-one injuries that year. Yogi Berra broke his thumb; Johnny Mize had a torn shoulder; Tommy Henrich fractured a bone in his back. The club might have quit almost anywhere along the line and been glad to finish in the first division. But Charles Dillon Stengel hadn't signed on to manage the Yankees home in fourth place, third place, or even second place. He intended to win, and he convinced his ballplayers, healthy, halt and lame, that the Yankees were going to win. When they did, he wasn't surprised. Nor did he forget to give a full measure of credit to Joe DiMaggio, whose electrifying comeback in mid-season picked the club up off the floor and started it on its way.

They forgot about McCarthy when Stengel's pennants began to pile up—1949, 1950, 1951, 1952, 1953, five in a row before the Indians beat him out in '54. Then back again in '55, '56, '57 and '58, out for a season in '59 when his old Dodger protégé, Al Lopez, who had beaten him with Cleveland in '54, did it again with Chicago, and back for a last bow in 1960. Ten American League pennants and seven world championships added up to a record unmatched by any other manager in the history of the game.

Out of all those pennants, all those "crucial" games, nothing stands out in memory quite so vividly as Casey and his 1958 Yankees doing battle with the Milwaukee Braves who had beaten them so soundly in the World Series of 1957. The Braves, proud and confident in their role of defending world champions, took the first two games on their own ground, 4–3 and 13–5. Back in Yankee Stadium, Don Larsen and Ryne Duren combined to shut out the Braves, 4–0, but it looked bad for the Yankees when old man Warren Spahn cranked out a 3–0 win for Milwaukee in the fourth game. All the Braves needed was one more victory to lock it up, and nobody doubted that they would get it. The Series had begun with two games in Milwaukee; the third, fourth and fifth games were scheduled for Yankee Stadium. If either a sixth or seventh game was required, they would be played in County Stadium, Milwaukee, but not many baseball men thought it would be necessary to make the trip back to the land of beer, cheese and *sauerbraten*. Because, if the Yankees won, we would have to fly back to Milwaukee about two hours after game five, all of us in the Series party had to bring our bags to Yankee Stadium that afternoon. I was out on the ball field during batting practice, talking to one of the veteran Yankee stars, and I asked him if he thought it was likely that we would be making the trip. He shook his head. "Not a chance," he said. "I wish I thought so, but I'm afraid their pitchers are just too much for our kids."

But the Yankees surprised everybody—everybody, that is, except Stengel—with a lopsided 7–0 victory behind Bob Turley's good pitching. All afternoon Casey was on his feet, urging his men on, pushing them, sometimes even dragging them bodily through inning after inning. Watching him, you got the impression that if they didn't think they could make it on their own he was ready to pick them up and carry them on his own wiry old shoulders. But if you felt that way on getaway day in the Bronx, the feeling was doubled in spades during the sixth game in Milwaukee. The Braves' fans were fast becoming famous for the silent treatment they gave the visiting teams in their handsome new ball park, and the New Yorkers, accustomed to giving a generous round of applause to every big hit or fine play by a visiting player, labeled such behavior strictly "bush." Usually the New York newspapermen are too sophisticated, too proud of their objectivity, to root openly for one of their teams, but they broke tradition in Milwaukee that fall. They banged their palms together and they whistled loud whistles and they grinned like a bunch of somewhat embarrassed fathers at a Little League game as the Yankees beat down Spahn, 4–3, to tie the Series at three games apiece.

After that, you knew the Yankees were going the rest of the way. The Braves must have known it, too; at least, they acted as if they did. There was an easy confidence about the Yankees when they went through their workout before the seventh game, and there was just as much ease and confidence about the way they won the game. Don Larsen, the starter, couldn't make it, but Bob Turley took over in the third inning and gave the Braves only two hits the rest of the way. Turley was the particular hero of the Series, the winner of the flashy new Chevrolet Corvette that *Sport* magazine gives away after the last game every fall, but the real hero was Stengel—and every man wearing a Yankee uniform knew it. None of the Yankees had given up when the Braves had run up their 3-to-1 lead in games, but neither had they really believed they had a chance to win. Casey not only didn't give up, he never stopped thinking he would win. Nobody who was with the Yankees in those games will ever forget the old man standing out on the top of the dugout steps pumping his arms like a boxer, yelling at everybody all at once, the men on the field and the men on the bench, insistent as a fire siren, demanding that they go get them, go get them, go get them.

That was Casey's last world championship but it was also his sweetest one, the one he cherished the most. He sat in the clubhouse in his old-fashioned long underwear for an hour and a half, savoring it. He talked to everybody who wanted to talk to him, he congratulated everybody who came near him, he drank his beer with the smacking lips of a man who has earned every wet, cold drop of it.

At the parties and the press conferences and the all-night bull sessions that went on after the Series, nobody stayed up later than Casey, nobody talked more baseball than Casey, nobody was funnier or made more sense or hammed it up better than Casey. He's a natural-born actor, a genius at pantomime, a stand-up comedian who writes his own material and a cracker-barrel philosopher whose homely truths come not out of somebody else's thinking but out of his own incredibly varied experience. No party can ever go dead when Casey Stengel is around. *Sports Illustrated*'s Gerald Holland once wrote about being at a Yankee celebration at which Casey heard somebody mention Bill Veeck's midget, Eddie Gaedel, who became a *cause célèbre* when Veeck signed him to a contract with the St. Louis Browns and actually had him get up to bat once (he walked, naturally) before the Commissioner put a stop to the experiment. "Midgets are smart," Casey declared in his inimitable out-of-the-blue fashion. "Smart, and as slick as eels. You know why? It's because they're not able to do much with the short fingers they have. You understand? Not being able to do much with their fingers, what do they do?" He tapped his forehead. "They developed their brainpower." That stopped his audience cold, but it didn't stop Casey. He went on like an express train, slowing down a little on the curves and picking up speed on the straightaways. "Short people tend to be smarter all along the line," he insisted. "You take bartenders. A short bartender will out-perform a tall bartender every time. You know why?" Nobody knew why except Casey. "Because," he said, "here's your tall bartender." He stood on tiptoe and began pouring imaginary drinks into imaginary glasses on an imaginary bar. "You get the idea?" he demanded, grimacing as if in pain and putting a hand to his back. "It gets him in the back. He gets a sore back, and he's out of there in a few hours." He straightened up. "Now, then, with your short bartender the bar is right at his shoulder level." Casey shot his arms straight out, whizzing them back and forth like pistons, working furiously to show a short bartender serving drinks by the dozen. "You get it?" he said triumphantly. "No back strain at all. He can go all night!"

Casey has a solution for every problem, including problems nobody else has thought of.

The Yankees blew the pennant in 1959 and the World Series in 1960 when a ball took a bad hop and hit Tony Kubek in the eye and allowed Bill Mazeroski to hit a decisive home run for the Pittsburgh Pirates in the seventh game, but none of that diminished Casey Stengel. He gave the Yankees the kind of generalship they had known in other times from Miller Huggins and Joe McCarthy. He was retired because the club was committed to a policy of bringing on younger men to fill the top jobs in the front office and in the dugout, but the remarkable performance he subsequently turned in as manager of the brand-new New York Mets simply proved all over again that Casey Stengel stands supreme as a baseball original. They don't make them like him any more.

They don't make them like Charlie Dressen, either, and that may

be a good thing for everybody, although when Charlie was appointed
manager of the Detroit Tigers in 1963 he seemed to have become
something perilously close to an organization man. The old, or
young, Dressen was interested in organizations only as they represented challenges to his rugged—if not rampant—individualism.
This is the kind of man Charlie was when he was a washed-up ballplayer looking around, in the summer of 1932, for a job as manager.
The banks were closing, war veterans were selling apples on every
corner, and Charlie didn't know any way to make a living except
baseball. He got a tip from a friend that the Nashville club of the
Southern Association was looking for a new manager, and he bor-
rowed enough money from the friend to go down there and apply
for the job. Fay Murray, the man who owned the club, had his
doubts. "How do I know you can do the job?" he wanted to know.
If Charlie was the kind of man who could be stopped by a question,
that might have stopped him or at least slowed him down. Instead,
he countered with a question of his own. "Mr. Murray," he said,
"exactly what do you expect from your manager this season?"

"Well," Murray said, considering, "we sure haven't done very
well so far this year. We're four games under .500 right now, 36
and 40, and I don't think it's too much to ask for a ball team to win
at least half its games, do you?" Dressen didn't. "I'll make a deal
with you," he said. "I'll play third base and manage your ball club
the rest of the way for you, and if I don't win half the games left on
the schedule, you don't have to pay me a nickel in salary. All you'll
be stuck for is my expenses, and you'll be getting a third baseman
for nothing in the deal."

Murray agreed, and he almost won the bet. Dressen took his ball
club into the last game of the season with a record under his
managership of 38 wins and 38 losses, knowing he had to win to
collect his pay. If he lost, he would end up below .500 and it would
be a long, cold winter for Charles Walter Dressen. "If ever a
manager tried to get a ball club 'up' for one big game," Charlie

said years later, "it was me that day. We finally won it, something like 11–7 or 12–8, but I really worked for it. Imagine having your whole season's salary riding on one ball game."

Actually, according to what Murray said later, he intended to pay Charlie anyway, but he definitely hadn't made up his mind to rehire him for the next season until he saw the nervy way Charlie came through in the clutch. A good football quarterback with the famous Staley Starch Company team, one of the big names of pro football's pioneer days, and a thoroughly competent infielder for seven seasons with the Cincinnati Reds (his lifetime batting average as a major-leaguer was .272), Charlie always was a fiery competitor. Like a lot of small men, he made up for his lack of size with his aggressiveness and his attention to detail. Those were the qualities that made him a good manager and that convinced Fay Murray he ought to give Charlie the Vols for the full season of 1933. The owner had no cause to regret it. Dressen had the club in contention most of the summer and finished a respectable third. Things seemed to be going well for him, and then, all of a sudden, they began to go even better. The New York Giants, driving hard for the National League pennant, had a working agreement with Nashville, and when Johnny Vergez, their third baseman, was taken out of the lineup by appendicitis, they asked for Charlie. He got into sixteen games for the Giants as they nailed down the pennant, and although it's unlikely that his .222 batting average or his three runs-batted-in had any appreciable effect on the outcome, he did wear the Giant uniform long enough to add another chapter to the growing legend of Dressen the quick thinker, the master strategist and the bold gambler. That happened in the World Series against the Washington Senators.

The Giants, with Carl Hubbell pitching, were nursing a 2–1 lead in the last half of the eleventh inning of the fourth game, at Washington. They led in the Series, two games to one, and would be off and running if they could hold on to this one. Fred Schulte singled,

Joe Kuhel beat out a bunt and Ossie Bluege moved up both runners with a sacrifice, giving the Senators men on second and third with one out. Bill Terry, the great first baseman and manager of the Giants, ordered Hubbell to walk Luke Sewell, the Washington catcher, intentionally, so the bases were loaded when big Cliff Bolton, a reserve catcher, came up to pinch-hit. Bolton was a dangerous left-handed hitter whose batting average in thirty-three games for Washington was a frightening .410. It didn't look good for the Giants. Terry prudently ordered his infield to play in tight and try to cut off the run at the plate. But Bill had barely motioned his fielders in when Charlie Dressen bounded out of the Giants' dugout and ran onto the field. "You can get two on this guy, Bill," he said excitedly. "I know him from the Association. Pull the infield back for the double play and pitch him high and outside." That didn't sound so good to Terry. "That's really asking for it," he said doubtfully. "We pitch him high and outside like that and he hits a fly ball and the ball game is all tied up. We better pitch him low and make him hit it on the ground." Anybody else would have shrugged his shoulders at that point and retreated with honor back to the dugout. But Charlie Dressen is made of sterner stuff. Sticking his neck out is the only way he knows how to live. "I'm telling you," he insisted, "I know him. He swings down on the ball. And he's so slow he couldn't beat his grandmother down to first. Pitch him high and outside and you'll get the double play." Terry was impressed. He was even more impressed when he did what Charlie wanted him to do and it worked out exactly as Charlie had said it would. Furthermore, being a rigidly honest man, Terry told one and all that it was Dressen's idea, and Charlie's reputation swelled.

One of the baseball men who heard the word was Larry MacPhail, the young, ambitious general manager of Dressen's old ball club, the Cincinnati Reds. When MacPhail decided to fire his manager, Bob O'Farrell, in the middle of the 1934 season he remembered Dressen and took a trip down to Nashville to see him in action as a manager.

He liked what he saw and asked Fay Murray if he would release
Charlie to take the Cincinnati job. Murray was reluctant but he
was also badly in need of a catcher, and when MacPhail offered to
give him a catcher off the Reds' roster in exchange for Dressen, he
shook hands with Charlie and wished him all the best.

It just isn't in Dressen to show awe in any situation but he was
thoroughly charged up by the knowledge that, at thirty-six, he was
one of the select group of sixteen major-league managers. In and out
of office (and over the years he has managed the Reds, Dodgers,
Senators, Braves and Tigers), he has stayed charged up. Some men
are born to fulfill a particular function, and Charlie Dressen was
born to be the manager of a baseball club in the major leagues. As
Everett McKinley Dirksen is at home in the Senate of the United
States, Charlie Dressen is at home in the dugout and the coaching
box. He didn't win any pennants with the Reds; he finished eighth,
sixth, fifth and then eighth again before Warren Giles, who had
succeeded MacPhail in the front office, decided it was time for the
inevitable change. But he gained the experience he needed to follow
the only career that interested him. He wasn't any longer "manage-
rial caliber," as the baseball writers like to label young men who
show signs of being able to think without pain; he was a professional
manager, eligible to take his place in the endless game of musical
chairs which all career managers must play because it is so much
cheaper to fire a manager than it is to build a better ball club.

Charlie may yet get his hands on a ball club that will allow him
to make a run at the records of the big winners like McGraw, Mack,
McCarthy and Stengel, but until he does it will stand in the books
that his glory years were the years in Brooklyn with Peewee Reese,
Jackie Robinson, Gil Hodges, Roy Campanella, Carl Furillo, Don
Newcombe, Carl Erskine, Duke Snider and the rest. That was the
perfect ball club for Dressen, in the perfect town for him. Charlie's
loquacity, and he can give aces and spades to the most compulsive
talkers the game has ever known and still be in there at the finish, a
little hoarse maybe but still game, didn't seem unusual to the

Brooklyn fans. They had just been weaned from Leo Durocher and
Branch Rickey. Some of his ballplayers offered a few hurt sugges-
tions that it might be nicer if he would say "we" once in a while
instead of "I" all the time, but that wasn't important. Charlie's "I"
is the "I" of the fight manager who substitutes his own identity for
that of his athlete at all times except the three minutes of the round
of boxing itself. He doesn't mean to take the credit away from his
ballplayers or steal the spotlight from them; it just works out that
way. Nevertheless, years after he had folded his tent and noisily
departed from Brooklyn because Walter O'Malley wouldn't give
him a two-year contract like the one the Giants had just given his
arch-rival, Durocher, and an expense account like Durocher's, the
old Dodger heroes, philosophical but candid in the years of their
retirement, held to a man to the conviction that Dressen was the
best of all their managers, better than Durocher and better than
Burt Shotton and better than Walter Alston. "I think Charlie
Dressen is the greatest manager I ever played for," Jackie Robinson
said. "Most of the things I learned about baseball I learned from
him. For me, the most important thing about being a manager is
staying a step or two ahead of the ball game. Dressen is a genius at
running over in his mind each possibility that might turn up next
and deciding which course he ought to follow in each case. He keeps
his eye on everything that happens on the ball field and he's always
ready for whatever might happen next. You hardly ever catch
Dressen by surprise. No matter what you do, you can bet he's been
thinking ahead of time about what he'll do if you do it."

It is a sad fact of history that Charlie's magnificent intellect did
not prevent some memorable catastrophes from overtaking the
Dodgers during the years of his regime. The worst, of course, was
The Home Run struck by Bobby Thomson to snatch the third game
of the extraordinary play-off series of 1951 out of the Dodgers'
hands and catapult the "miracle" Giants and their practically peer-
less leader, as Red Smith liked to call Durocher, into the World
Series. That may endure throughout the rest of Dressen's baseball

career as the blackest day of his life. But some of the days that preceded it, when the Dodgers were busy blowing what had been in midsummer a 13½-game lead, were dismal, too, and there were a few days in the early fall of 1952 and again in the fall of 1953—at World Series time, that is—that weren't especially happy either. Charlie lost the '52 Series in seven games and the '53 Series in six. He had survived the Thomson home run, he had survived the cliff-hanging Series in '52, he had even survived his famous misadventure into the world of grammar with his prediction in the middle of the 1953 season that "The Giants is dead," but Charlie couldn't quite survive the events that closed out the 1953 season—and his tenure in Brooklyn. The Brooklyn Board of Education came belatedly to Charlie's rescue in the furor over his grammar. "The manager is correct," a spokesman for the Board insisted. "You wouldn't say the United States *are* the best country in the world, would you? So how can you say 'The Giants *are* dead?' Maybe if one of the Giants was alive you might have a point, but none of them is, so 'The Giants is dead' is perfectly proper." But hardly anybody except his ball-players, who were generally ruled out as prejudiced witnesses, came to his defense after the first game of the 1953 Series in which he was twice outthought by Yogi Berra. Hardly anybody in Brooklyn could forgive him for that.

The Yankees got off to a 4–0 start in the first inning of that memorable game and added another run in the fifth when Berra hit a home run, but the Dodgers scored one run in the fifth on Jim Gilliam's homer and three in the sixth on a single by Billy Cox and home runs by Gil Hodges and pinch hitter George Shuba. The Dodger rooters in the big crowd of almost 70,000 sat up and yelled their heads off when their team went right to work again in the top of the seventh. Roy Campanella started it with a Texas League single to left. "The only mark they put in the book is that you got a single," Campy said, cheerfully accepting the blooper hit. Hodges hit a sharp grounder to Phil Rizzuto and it looked like a sure double-play ball, but Phil couldn't hold it and it went as a single. Carl Furillo promptly singled home Campanella and the Dodgers could taste the Yankees' blood. With Furillo on first, Hodges on second and nobody out, Dressen put on what all baseball men call "the bunt sign." In baseball, all signals are signs, and it is one of Charlie Dressen's proudest boasts that nobody in baseball is more skilled at stealing other people's signs than he is. This sign, however, was his own, and whether it was actually stolen or simply anticipated no longer matters. Whatever happened, the play it precipitated didn't work. Billy Cox, the Brooklyn third baseman and a good man on a bunt play, laid down a bunt in front of the plate. Yogi Berra pounced on it instantly, as though he had known exactly what was going to happen, and fired the ball to third base ahead of the hard-running Hodges. Artie Gore, a National League umpire, called Hodges out so quickly and so emphatically, although it was a breath-takingly close play, that some bitter critics said later that he had his hand up in the "out" gesture before either the runner or the ball had reached the base. Yogi had taken a daring chance throwing to third instead of making the safe play at first, but the gamble had worked. One angry Dodger fan said after the game, "The only reason Yogi threw to third was that he could see Gore had already called Hodges out." It was a great play for the Yankees and a backbreaking blow to the Dodgers. When Yogi followed it up by a carbon-copy play, picking up Clem Labine's bunt and firing the ball right back to Gil McDougald at third to get Furillo, it was almost an anticlimax. The damage had already been done. The Dodgers were out of the ball game, and as it turned out they were out of the Series. They never fully recovered and never made quite the fight of it that they had the year before.

Managers who have put two league championships back to back don't get fired every day, so it was a considerable surprise when Walter O'Malley gently separated Dressen from his job during the winter. Not many of the press corps covering the Dodgers took

O'Malley seriously when he said that the only difference between him and the manager was that Charlie wanted a two-year contract and that, much as they wanted to give it to him, club policy was against it. Most of them were convinced that the trouble was more elementary; Charlie had forgotten to beat the Yankees.

If beating the Yankees was an absolute qualification for holding a job as manager in the American League, one of the few men still young enough to work at the trade who would be eligible is Al Lopez. In the long span of years from 1949 through 1963, Al was the only non-Yankee manager to enjoy the satisfaction of winning the pennant. Al managed the Cleveland Indians to the championship in 1954 and did it again in 1959 with the Chicago White Sox. He couldn't beat the National League either time in the World Series, losing first to the Giants and then to the Dodgers, but at least he proved that the Yankees can be beaten once in a while, if not often.

Al is one of those rare ballplayers who are looked upon as potential managers even while they are still going strong on the ball field. Because of the nature of his job, his heavy responsibilities in calling pitches, setting up defensive alignments and relaying signs, almost every outstanding catcher attracts a certain amount of attention as a possible manager. This is especially true if the catcher's personality and character seem to fit the blueprint of the ideal manager, if there is such a thing. When you think about Lopez and the other first-class managers of his time, Stengel, Durocher, Dressen, Alston and Houk, you have to conclude that there isn't. From Stengel at one extreme to Lopez at the other, they are wildly different.

Like Alston, Lopez is a low-pressure manager. He has always believed that he manages best who manages least. He reminded me of Bucky Walters when he said in his slow, serious way, "All the managers know baseball pretty good, you know." (He's like Dressen, at least, in his easy, uninhibited approach to the rules of grammar.) "You're not going to outsmart anybody very often in this league."

He doesn't go in much for clubhouse meetings, either the revival-meeting or the chalk-talk kind. "I attended hundreds of those meetings when I was playing ball," he says, "and most of them were pure and simple a waste of time." It is typical of Lopez that he doesn't like to ask his ballplayers to do anything that he resented being asked—or told—to do when he was a player. There isn't a more courteous, thoughtful or understanding man in the game. When his Cleveland club was massacred by the Giants in the '54 Series, on the wings of those devastating Fu Manchu home runs in the Polo Grounds by Dusty Rhodes, the reporters assigned to the losers' clubhouse felt so badly for Al that they hated to add to his misery by asking him the foolish questions they were bound by tradition to ask. They glared at the photographer whose bad taste extended to asking the manager to pose with his head in his hands. Al tried it briefly, then straightened up. "That's too uncomfortable," he said. "If you just need a sad picture, you shouldn't have any trouble getting it. Not if I look the way I feel."

Fortunately for Al, there have been a lot of good days along with the inevitable bad ones in his long baseball career. He was a seventeen-year-old kid catching for Jacksonville in the Florida State League when he caught Wilbert Robinson's eye by belting a screaming triple off Dazzy Vance in his first time up against the great left-hander in an exhibition game against the Dodgers. He caught on as a regular with the Dodgers in 1930 and lasted for eighteen seasons as a catcher in the big leagues. He always says that if he had had to earn his keep as a hitter he would have starved to death, but his lifetime batting average of .261 isn't bad for a catcher —and Lopez was one of the best catchers of his day. His ability to make the bunt play, and to get down to first and third to back up throws there, won him the reputation of being a fifth infielder. "But that," he says with his easy Castilian laugh, "didn't keep Casey Stengel from trading me away twice. He traded me off the Brooklyn ball club in 1935 and off Boston in 1940. I remember, the first time he traded me I was up in New York on a business trip and it was during the off-season and I was going to have dinner with a few friends. We were having a drink in my hotel room before we went out, and the phone rang, and it was Casey. He wanted to know if he could come up for a few minutes, and naturally I said sure, come ahead. Well, you know Casey. He talked for three hours straight before we finally went out for something to eat, and by the time we got back to the hotel it was two o'clock in the morning. I was just getting ready to fall into bed when the phone rang and it was Casey again, and he wanted to come up again. I didn't know how to say no to him, so I told him to come on up, and when he came in he said, 'Al, it's just that I've got to tell you I think we're going to have to trade you. The club's in trouble and we've got to make a deal. Everybody wants either Mungo or you, and we can't trade Mungo because he's the drawing card. So I guess it'll have to be you. But I want you to know I'll see to it that you go to a good ball club.' I said, 'Thanks, Case, I appreciate it.' I did, too. It was nice of him to worry about me like that, he didn't have to do it. But I didn't appreciate it quite so much when I got back to Ybor City, which is in Tampa, where I live, and I found out from the papers that I had been traded to the Boston Braves. This was what Casey meant by a good club? They had lost 115 ball games the year before and it wasn't until Casey had the Mets for their first season in 1962 that anybody broke that record. I saw Case one day that spring in Clearwater, where the Dodgers were training, and I told him I was real glad he had taken care to send me to a good ball club, otherwise I might have ended up in Keokuk. Then, sonofagun if he didn't get another chance to trade me, five years later, when he was managing Boston, and this time he sends me to Pittsburgh. They were in last place when he sent me there, and I guess that just goes to show you what Casey Stengel considers a good ball club."

All the time he was bouncing around the league, from the Dodgers to the Braves to the Pirates, Al was learning the game. He was learning about handling pitchers, about encouraging the faint-hearted and about disciplining the overconfident ballplayers. By the time he caught on with the Cleveland Indians for the 1947 season, Al was beginning to think seriously of a career as a manager. He wasn't the only one thinking about it for him. Bill Veeck, who had taken over the Cleveland ball club, lock, stock and barrel, was making no secret of his conviction that Lou Boudreau, who had come with the franchise, was a million-dollar shortstop and a ten-cent manager. During the winter between the seasons of '47 and '48, Veeck set up a deal with the St. Louis Browns which would have sent Boudreau, outfielder Dick Kokos and pitcher Red Embree to St. Louis in exchange for shortstop Vern Stephens, outfielder Paul Lehner and pitcher Jack Kramer. The heart of the deal, Boudreau for Stephens, made sense only if you shared Veeck's conviction that Louie was a handicap to the ball club as manager and that the combination of a new manager and a shortstop replacement as solid as Stephens, who could swing a pretty hot bat, was worth more than Boudreau, the best shortstop and one of the most inspirational players in the game, and Boudreau the sometimes inept manager. Veeck sent up a trial balloon by leaking word of the trade to a couple of his friends among the Cleveland newspapermen, and he made ready for the deal—if he should decide to go ahead with it—by reaching a provisional agreement with Al Lopez that Al would manage the ball club for him.

It all fell through, unfortunately for Al but fortunately for the outcome of the Cleveland pennant bid that year, when the baseball fans of the city, aroused by the warning headlines of the impending deal, revolted. They drew up petitions, clogged the Cleveland Stadium switchboard with protesting telephone calls, sent angry telegrams by the thousands, set up booths on downtown streets to distribute postcard protests ready for mailing, and in short did everything but run Veeck out of town on a rail with the traditional tar and feathers. Lou Boudreau was their hero, their white knight,

their Sir Lancelot, and they weren't about to see this carpetbagger
Veeck come in and take him away from them. So Al Lopez didn't
get the job Veeck wanted him to have and went instead to Indianapolis of the American Association for his first shot at managing.
Lou Boudreau stayed in Cleveland, hit .355 for the Indians, played
shortstop like the second coming of Honus Wagner, and led the
club to the pennant by beating Boston in a special play-off in which
he personally struck two home runs and two singles in four times
at bat.

Lopez didn't have such a bad year himself. He won the pennant
with Indianapolis and demonstrated to everybody's satisfaction that
Veeck had picked out a 14-karat, solid-gold prospect for the very
special function of managing a baseball club in the major leagues.
One of those who was satisfied was Hank Greenberg, who had been
a special assistant to Veeck in the Cleveland front office and had
succeeded him as general manager when Bill sold out his interest in
the club and went through the capital-gain hocus-pocus that made
him a millionaire. Greenberg went along with Boudreau through
the 1950 season but that was as far as he was willing to go. The
people still loved Louie in Cleveland, as they still love him today,
and Greenberg didn't risk sending up any trial balloons about his
plans. He simply announced that he was hiring Al Lopez to manage
the Indians in 1951 and 1952 and that in recognition of his great
contributions to Cleveland baseball Lou Boudreau had been given
his unconditional release and was free to make a deal for himself and
to keep all the proceeds from it. It was a neat way of minimizing
the barrage of criticism that Hank knew would break over his head,
and as much as any plan could that had to deal with such a difficult
situation it worked. Boudreau was sought by at least half the clubs
in the majors—his batting average had slipped to .269 in 1950 but
he could still play a lot of shortstop and he was a big drawing card
all around the league. Furthermore, he might again come in handy
as a manager. The Yankees, Senators and Red Sox made him the

most tempting offers, and he finally signed with the Rex Sox, partly because it was his shrewd guess that there, where Steve O'Neill, an old hand at the musical chairs game, was on shaky ground, he would have his best chance of reclaiming his manager's card. That's the way it worked out. After two seasons with the Red Sox, Lou became their manager.

Lopez lasted six years as manager of the Indians and it is a tribute to the affection that he has felt for Casey Stengel over the years since he first played for him in Brooklyn that Al can even bear to hear Casey's name mentioned without breaking out in a cold sweat. In his six seasons in Cleveland, Al finished second to the Stengel Lancers five times. Once, in 1954, he beat them—and he had to win 111 games to do it because the Yankees, finishing second, won 103, the most any of Casey's Yankee teams ever won. It was a particularly sweet victory for Lopez because Stengel had gone out on a limb right after his club had wrapped up the 1953 Series and predicted that they would do it again the next year. "My team is just growing into greatness," he said cockily, "and it will win again." But the Indians held up all season, and on September 12 they torpedoed the Yankees in both ends of a doubleheader at Cleveland Stadium to make it official. Except for the day Lou Boudreau's gang beat the Red Sox in the 1948 play-off, that was the best day Cleveland baseball ever knew. There were 86,583 people in the stands to watch Bob Lemon win his 22nd game of the season in the first game, 4–1, with a six-hitter, and Early Wynn pick up No. 21 in the second game, 3–2, with a three-hitter. The cold beer Al Lopez drank in the clubhouse after that doubleheader was the best beer he ever drank in his life. The fact that his old tormentor, Stengel, was in such a fury that he wouldn't even let any newspapermen into his club's dressing room didn't make the good-natured Cleveland manager feel any worse.

It was a tough break for Al that he couldn't make off with a single game in the Series. It was bad enough to be beaten by the

Giants, but to go down in four straight, with strong-armed pitchers like Lemon and Wynn and Mike Garcia going for you, was hard to take.

Al was in Chicago when he got his next shot at the Series. He came up a winner for Bill Veeck in 1959 and faced Walter Alston's Los Angeles Dodgers in the Series. He had a right to be hopeful when his White Sox won the first game in a walk, 11–0, with Ted Kluszewski, the muscular retread from Cincinnati, hitting a couple of home runs. But the Dodgers came on to win the next three in a row, getting good pitching in tight ball games, and although the White Sox had enough moxie to win a tough fifth game, 1–0, they couldn't go any further. It wasn't the fault of Alfonso Ramon Lopez, though. Managers don't come any better than this man. The Cleveland ballplayers bought him an expensive set of matched golf clubs as a going-away present when he emptied out his locker to make the move to Chicago, and that's a gesture about as rare in big-league baseball as the players chipping in for a birthday present for the owner. They did it because they knew what they were losing.

One of the most successful managers of recent years was so little known when he moved into his job that hardly anybody except a few men in the front office knew what the ball club was getting in him. That would be Walter Alston, the surprise choice of Walter O'Malley and his general manager, Buzzy Bavasi, to succeed Charlie Dressen after the great contract dispute that bounced Charlie all the way back to Oakland in the Pacific Coast League. Alston owned one line in the Official Encyclopedia of Baseball because he had got up to bat once for the St. Louis Cardinals in a 1936 ball game with the Chicago Cubs (he struck out), but other than that he was as much of a stranger to the radio-, television- and newspapermen as he was to the fans. The day he was presented to the press as the new Brooklyn manager, a clerk in an office across the alley from the Dodgers' offices attracted the attention of one of the reporters and held up a banner inquiring, "Cookie?" Apparently the curious fan thought Cookie Lavagetto was the best bet to take over from

Dressen. The reporter shook his head and reached for a piece of typewriter paper. He printed ALSTON on it in big block letters and held it out the window. The clerk disappeared for a minute and then came back holding up another sign, asking plaintively, "Who's Alston?"

A week or so after his appointment Walter accepted an invitation from the publishers of *Sport* magazine to attend a luncheon at Toots Shor's. Nobody from the Dodger front office was with him when he arrived at the restaurant because he had been delayed while he took care of some personal business in midtown. He stood at the bar, unrecognized, next to Lou Boudreau and Casey Stengel, for a good quarter of an hour before one of the magazine's editors, acting on a hunch, asked if he wasn't Walter Alston and introduced him to his fellow major-league managers. As late as September in his first season in Brooklyn, Walter was sitting in the dugout with a group of his players during batting practice when a photographer approached him and asked loudly, "Mister, can you tell me which one's Alston?" The players laughed, and Walter, who carries a lot of quiet dignity in his big body, smiled gently. "Oh," he said, "I guess he's around somewhere."

Alston has been in baseball, one way or another, for a long time, but nobody in New York had bothered to follow his steps from Greenwood in the East Dixie League to Montreal in the International League, where he managed the Triple-A Royals for four seasons before getting the call to Brooklyn. He began managing at Portsmouth, Virginia, in 1940, led to it by the collapse of his hopes for a career as a major-league ballplayer and a determination to find a place for himself somewhere in the game. He was an off-season schoolteacher in his home town, Darrtown, Ohio, because, as he put it, "When you're in the minors you don't make much money." But it wasn't easy for him to keep up two careers. "The trouble was," he says, "they overlapped. Whenever I took a teaching job I'd tell the school superintendent or the principal that I had a baseball job, too, and that I would have to leave when the ball season opened. So they had to get a substitute for me every spring, and after a while they got tired of it. In fact, to be blunt about it, they fired me."

Once he had made his way up to the higher classifications of the minors, first with St. Paul of the American Association and then with Montreal, Alston didn't have to worry about teaching biology, science, or industrial arts. Even top minor-league managers don't get rich on their salaries but they do make a decent living and Walter Alston is a plain man who doesn't require silk pajamas à la Leo Durocher or gourmet meals à la Charlie Dressen. He was doing what he wanted to do and he was satisfied. Whether he ever dreamed about moving to Ebbets Field and managing the Dodgers, Walter never has said. But there is no question that he was ready and willing to handle the assignment when it was offered to him. He never considered passing it up. Alston is shy, but he's not that shy.

"At least we've got the percentages on our side," he said when he met the Brooklyn players at Vero Beach in the spring of 1954. "This club has been in a few World Series but hasn't won one yet. Of course," he grinned slowly, "we've got to win the pennant first." He didn't make it that first year, and a lot of the fans wanted his scalp. They thought he was too conservative, not only in the way he dressed and the way he saved his words as though they were dollar bills, but in the way he ran his ball games, too. They blamed him for holding down the larcenous Brooklyn base runners to the extent that the 90 stolen bases they had racked up under Dressen in 1953 dwindled to only 46 in 1954. Under Alston the Dodgers used the hit-and-run less, seldom went for the extra base, lost their enthusiasm for challenging outfielders' throwing arms, and worst of all, argued among themselves about whether or not the new manager was hurting the ball club.

Things happened like the time Duke Snider hit a ball into the bleachers in left-center field at Wrigley Field in Chicago. The ball bounced off the body of a spectator, standing inside the center-field wall, and caromed back on the field. The umpires, hesitantly, ruled it a double. Jackie Robinson promptly ran out onto the field and began to argue the point. He argued strenuously, even violently, until all of a sudden he realized that he was all alone out there. He looked over toward third base, and there, in the coaching box, was Alston, making no move to join the party. Plainly embarrassed, Jackie headed back to the dugout. Later, talking to the interviewers pressing him hard in the clubhouse, he said, "That's the last time I'll argue over any play I'm not directly involved in myself. From now on, I'll leave the fighting up to the manager." The manager was equally candid. "I just didn't see the ball," he said. "I didn't argue because I wasn't sure, to tell you the truth, if the ball had cleared the wall or not."

That kind of thing hurt Alston badly in Brooklyn—until he won the World Series in 1955. Wilbert Robinson had won a pennant in 1920, Leo Durocher had won one in 1941, Burt Shotton had won in 1947 and 1949, and Charlie Dressen had won in 1952 and 1953, but none of them had been able to go on and win the World Series. In 1955 Walter Alston, sometimes ridiculed as "the wooden Indian manager," did. Nobody, including Walter, claimed that he did it alone. There was Jackie Robinson's dramatic steal of home in the first game which kept the Dodgers alive and fighting despite their 6–5 defeat; there was the fine pitching of Johnny Podres in games three and seven; there was the power hitting of Duke Snider and the clutch hitting of Gil Hodges; and there was the key play by Sandy Amoros that robbed Yogi Berra of an extra-base hit and the Yankees of the tying runs in the seventh game. Right down to the last play of the last game, when Peewee Reese picked up Elston Howard's ground ball and threw it to Gil Hodges at first base for the last out, all the Dodgers gave it all they had. But Walter Alston, the man they had said was too conservative and too colorless ever to take the Dodgers all the way, had done the job. What Wilbert Robinson and Leo Durocher and Burt Shotton and Charlie Dressen hadn't been able to do, he had done.

Walter couldn't quite repeat in 1956, although he made it two National League pennants in a row, but he came up with his second world championship in 1959 with the Los Angeles Dodgers and he survived a couple of disappointing seasons to do it again for the rabid Los Angeles fans in 1963, proving that with Alston you never have to wait more than four years for a World Series win.

It hasn't been easy for Walter. He just hasn't got the kind of personality the press and the fans think a Dodger manager ought to have, which is probably just another way of saying that he isn't a Durocher or a Dressen. Then, for much of his career, he was paired off against Casey Stengel, which didn't help any. He had a good ball club to run, and when it went well, everybody said it was in spite of him; when it went badly, everybody said it was because of him. Because there isn't an ounce of pop-off in him, Alston never has fought back on either count. Nor has he ever done any electioneering with his ballplayers. He treats them as he thinks well-paid employees ought to be treated, in a businesslike, fair-minded, no-nonsense way. Dick Young of the New York *Daily News* put it this way: "There are guys like Harry Wismer who will bounce into an office building and say to the elevator operator, 'You're doing a grand job.' Then there are guys like Walter Alston who wouldn't say 'Nice work' to Dr. Albert Schweitzer." Alston, Dick said, "is the strong, silent type. He is Gary Cooper and John Wayne and Ben Casey. He does his job without acclaim, and he expects everyone else on the Dodgers to do his job—without so much as a grunt of recognition from him. There are a lot of people like Walter Alston. If they are pleased with you, they don't say a word. They take it for granted that you know how they feel about you. A kid doesn't wake up in the morning asking his father if he loves him, does he? He knows it without hearing it. He knows the old man would do anything in the world for him. That's how Walter Alston looks at life. There are some things that just don't have to be said."

But Walter's calm, cool approach to his job hasn't won him any easy medals. He has earned his good salary, won his rare awards and engraved his name in the record book by hard work, determination and a stubborn refusal ever to admit that he was beaten. Other managers have been successful with different qualities, but these are the weapons that took Walter Alston where he wanted to go.

In some respects, though not all, Ralph Houk of the Yankees resembles Alston. Ralph is more of an organization man than an individualist, a fact Dan Topping showed he appreciated when, at the end of the 1963 season, he promoted him to the post of general manager. It would have been hard for the Yankees to have found anyone more different in personality and character from Casey Stengel when they were looking for someone to succeed the Old Man. Stengel has always been willing to put the knock on his ball-players if he thought it would do them and the ball club some good; Houk never has anything but good to say about his players. Stengel seizes the center of the stage as naturally as he breathes; Houk likes to stay in the background and turn the spotlight on the men who do the pitching, the fielding and the hitting. Stengel enjoys letting the world know that he will take on the bosses in the front office any time he feels like it; Houk has no objection to everybody's knowing that he is a company man all the way.

One reporter, somewhat reluctantly nominating Houk for the 1963 Manager of the Year award, said: "Houk doesn't get his name in the paper a lot and he will never be accused of being a phrase-maker. This is a lack in the manager of a baseball team, who must be a lot of things, including public relations man. Yet by his own lights, and those of his employers, he gets the job done. He wins without the star players who are supposed to be the making of a manager. He looks down the bench and comes up with people who can do the job. For over a year John Blanchard couldn't do anything for Houk. But the Yankee manager never quite gave up on him and in the end Blanchard was a saver. His players rally around Houk like kids around a Good Humor man. They praise him for his toughness and his gentleness, for his firmness and for his under-standing. Mark Freeman, a pitcher who used to play for Houk in Denver, was a Stadium visitor one day and he put it this way: 'Houk is one of the few men who can walk the thin line, who can be familiar with his players and still command their respect. You can have a beer with Houk but you never forget he's the manager.' "

Houk isn't the kind of man you would ever be likely to disregard or even take lightly. The Yankee ballplayers didn't root for him to take over Stengel's job because they thought he would be a pushover as the boss. Most of them had known him for a long time, either as their manager at Denver or as their teammate on the Yankees. They knew him for a guy from Kansas with no nonsense about him, a guy who liked to smoke big cigars, liked to kid around, liked everybody to like him but would get his back up in a minute if anybody tried to push him around, a guy who could take care of himself with anybody up to—and, they were willing to bet, even including—Rocky Marciano. They had always, from his rookie days with the Yankees, called him the Major, or Maje, partly because he was an honest-to-God combat soldier in the 9th Armored Division reconnaissance group, with a Silver Star and a whole lot of dead Germans to his credit, and partly because he was promoted to major when he was discharged at the end of the war. Actually, as Ralph is quick to tell you, the last rank he held on active duty was captain, but to the Yankees he is the major, and it's a title that suits him admirably.

Ralph didn't think he had a chance of sticking with the big club in 1947, his first year back from the army, but he did, along with catchers Aaron Robinson, Gus Niarhos and rookie Yogi Berra. He didn't think he would be sent down in 1948, but he was, to Kansas City. He didn't think the Yankees would keep him on the club unless they intended to play him pretty frequently, but they did. He was with the club for five full seasons and parts of three others, during which he appeared in 91 games and made 43 hits for a batting average of .272. He was a World Series eligible six times but his total Series playing time consists of two times at bat, with one single, for a .500 average. "I was photographed," he likes to say, "once a year, for the team picture."

But whether he was sitting in the dugout with Casey Stengel or in the bullpen with the relief pitchers or making one of his rare appearances as a player, Ralph was endlessly studying the game. He began thinking about managing as early as his third or fourth year with the Yankees, and by the time his number was up as a player he was ready to start his new career. The Yankees thought enough of him to give him their prize Denver farm club in 1955. In Denver Ralph brought along some of the organization's most valuable prospects, youngsters like Tony Kubek, Bobby Richardson, Johnny Blanchard, Norm Siebern, Ryne Duren and Ralph Terry. He took on the job of coaxing Don Larsen to pitch the way everybody knew he was capable of pitching. He won the Little World Series in 1957, and the next year he was back in Yankee Stadium as Casey Stengel's first-base coach.

When Dan Topping and Del Webb, the co-owners of the Yankees, decided that for the good of the ball club they ought to move up younger men to replace general manager George Weiss and field manager Casey Stengel at the end of the 1960 season, despite the fact that the Weiss-Stengel combination had won another American League pennant in 1960 and lost the World Series to the Pittsburgh Pirates only after seven wild games, it was Ralph Houk they picked to move into Stengel's office. Roy Hamey, the man who had been earmarked to take over from Weiss, called Ralph one morning in October and asked him to come to Del Webb's suite in the Waldorf-Astoria at noon. There Ralph met both Webb and Topping, as well as Hamey, and was told that he was their choice to manage the club. It didn't take him long to agree to take the job, and an hour or so later he was introduced to the press at the Savoy-Hilton Hotel as the successor to Miller Huggins, Joe McCarthy and Casey Stengel.

Not all the newspapermen were happy about the way Casey had been eased out. Casey wasn't happy about it at all and he didn't mind saying so. He had a lot of old friends, and good friends, among the writers, and it was understandable that they should stand up for him. That didn't make Houk's job any easier. But he had the players on his side, which meant a lot, and he had the priceless assets of his own personality and character. He had never backed away from a fight in his life. He didn't back away from this one, and by the time October had come around again, he had won both the pennant and the World Series. Along the way, with him in charge, Roger Maris set a new major-league record by hitting 61 home runs, Whitey Ford won 25 ball games, and the Yankees looked like the Yankees. "This," Mickey Mantle said at the end of the season, "is the happiest club I've ever been on." The way Ralph won again in 1962 and 1963, to make it three for three, proved to the whole world that he had what it takes, but to the Yankee owners, to the ballplayers and to the writers who cover the club, it was Ralph's performance that first difficult season that meant the most. If they hadn't liked his nickname just the way it was, they would have commissioned him a general on the spot.

Things, in fact, went so well for Ralph Houk during his three-year hitch as the Yankees' manager, despite the almost continuous parade of crippled ballplayers he had to cope with, that he probably couldn't really appreciate what Al Lopez meant when he was discussing the business of managing with a newspaperman looking for an idea for a column. "Major-league ball is such a big business, Al," the writer said, "I've often wondered, can it still be fun, too?" Al leaned his head back against the dugout wall and looked the way a man looks when he's remembering happy times. "Man," he said softly, "I loved playing ball. I always had a lot of fun."

The writer picked him up quickly. "What about managing?" he wanted to know. "Don't you have any fun as a manager?"

Al said it for all managers, for all the ulcers and all the angry blowups with umpires and all the headaches, all the heartbreaking one-run defeats in the last of the ninth, all the mid-season firings. "Hell, no," he said, and it was said from the heart.

Chapter 10

Casey, do you think this was the best game Larsen
ever pitched?—UNIDENTIFIED SPORTSWRITER

IN all the years I've been broadcasting Yankee baseball games, there have been three individual accomplishments of
such walloping importance that they make all the others, all the
tape-measure home runs and miracle catches and dramatic no-hit
games, take a back seat. Joe DiMaggio's 56-game hitting streak was
one. The others were Don Larsen's Perfect Game and Roger Maris'
61 home runs in one season. The game will never be so old that the
people who follow it will stop talking about these three electrifying
performances, the last two just five years apart, one as sudden and
stunning as a bolt of lightning and the other as melodramatic and
unbearably suspenseful as a murder trial.

The 1956 World Series was all even at two games apiece when
Don Larsen walked to the mound at Yankee Stadium on the afternoon of October 8 to begin the fifth game by pitching to the
Brooklyn Dodgers' lead-off man, Jim Gilliam. Larsen had been
knocked out by the Dodgers in the second game of the Series; he
had lasted only two innings and his new "no-windup" delivery
hadn't been much of a mystery to the Brooklyn hitters. But this

was another day, and another chance, and although nobody who knew him would be likely to describe Larsen as the most serious-minded ballplayer around, he was entirely serious about taking every advantage he could of this second chance. He knew that George Weiss and Casey Stengel had their doubts about him and he wanted to be back at the Stadium in line for another World Series check next season.

One reason why Don was edgy about his future with the ball club was the trouble he had got into during spring training in Florida. He had had the bad luck to drive his car into one of the city of St. Petersburg's sturdiest telephone poles, and the pole hadn't yielded an inch. Don wasn't hurt, but because the Yankees had a midnight curfew—the accident happened at 5:30 in the morning—and Don's reputation as a fun-loving type was such that one of his nicknames was "The Nightrider," there was no reason for him to suspect that the widely publicized accident had done anything to endear him to the front office. Stengel hadn't punished him at the time, but Larsen knew as well as everybody else on the ball club that Casey had a long memory. He also knew that the best way to get in good with the Old Man was to pitch winning baseball, and that wasn't the kind of ball he had pitched against the Dodgers a few days ago.

Don had known since the previous afternoon, right after the Yankees had tied the Series by winning the fourth game, that he was going to pitch this one. Stengel had said so in the clubhouse. Don had welcomed the news and had thought about it off and on during a pleasant Sunday evening. He was out with his good friend Artie Richman, a baseball writer for the New York *Daily Mirror*. They drank a few bottles of beer together at the bar Bill Taylor, the old Giant outfielder, owned in Manhattan, and then took a cab back to the Bronx. Don was living at the Concourse Plaza Hotel just up the street from the Stadium. Sitting in the cab, he and Artie talked about who was in the running up to now for the $5,000 Chevy Corvette to be given away after the last game to the outstanding player in the Series. "That would be a hell of a thing to win," Larsen said. Then he laughed. "Who knows, maybe *I'll* win it? Maybe I'll beat Maglie tomorrow and hit a grand slam. Listen, don't laugh, if I ever get into one of those sliders of his, it just might go all the way." He thought about how nice that would be and it all seemed very possible. "What the hell," he said, kidding himself as much as Artie, "I might even pitch a no-hitter." So he got out of the taxicab in front of the hotel, bought himself a pizza pie and a morning paper, ordered a beer from room service, and went up to his room. He finally fell asleep at about one o'clock in the morning. Anyway, that's what Don says he did that night, and you had better believe him.

So there was Larsen with his 11–5 record on the season and his new idea not to wind up before delivering the ball, getting ready to pitch to Gilliam. "Very erratic," the magazine *Sports Illustrated* had said about him in its World Series scouting report, "but tougher than nails when right. Big, hard-throwing fastballer who can over-power the hitter but does not depend on speed alone; has good slider, throws occasional knuckler, this year developed an effective change of pace. Temperamental and sometimes rattles easily." Don looked in at Gilliam and began to work. He threw five pitches to Junior before he caught him looking at a 3-and-2 curve, fast and low, over the inside corner. Umpire Babe Pinelli of the National League, working behind the plate, said later that right then and there he thought to himself, Oh, oh, Larsen's really got it today.

He did have it. He used exactly 97 pitches to retire all 27 Dodger hitters, three up and three down every inning for nine innings. The only time he went to three balls all day was on the number two hit-ter in the first inning, Peewee Reese, and then he got Reese to strike out. After that, his control never gave him any trouble, and in fact he didn't give the impression of working hard at all. "Pitching quickly to the hitters," one writer said, "without a windup, he looked like a big kid throwing stones at a tin can in his back yard."

There were a few tense moments, although the first one wasn't really tense because at that point nobody knew how much it meant.

That was in the second inning when Jackie Robinson rapped a hot liner to the left side of the infield. It looked like a sure hit but Andy Carey, the Yankees' third baseman, jumped way up for it and got enough of his glove on it to deflect it over toward Gil McDougald at short. McDougald pounced on it and threw Robinson out by a step. Then in the fifth Gil Hodges caught hold of one and drove it deep to left-center field. Mickey Mantle had to run at top speed to catch up to the ball and even then he had to make a one-handed grab to make the out. Minutes later, Sandy Amoros poled a long drive into the seats in left, foul by inches. In the eighth, Andy Carey went barreling to his left to make a one-handed stab of Gil Hodges' low line drive, and you could hear every pair of lungs in the ball park gasp on that one. By then even the "clients" in the expensive box seats who traditionally go to the Series only to see and be seen, to be able to say they were there and not because they know or care anything about baseball, were aware that something big was happening.

"What a spot for the plate umpire to be on," Babe Pinelli said. "If I called a base on balls, it would go down in history as the Crime of the Century."

"I never had so many assistant managers in my life," Casey Stengel said. "Every time Larsen got ready to throw a pitch the guys on the bench were hollering out to the fielders, telling them where to play the hitter."

The official scorekeepers in the press box, Lyall Smith, Gus Steiger and Jerry Mitchell, showed in their faces the apprehension they felt that they might have to rule "hit" or "error" on one that could be called either way. And all of us in the broadcasting booth had to wrestle with the problem of how to inform our audience of fifty million or so people what was going on without violating the ancient baseball taboo against mentioning a no-hitter out loud before it is an accomplished fact.

"They're still in the game," Yogi Berra told Don in his practical

way when they went out for the top of the ninth. "Let's get the first
guy. That's the main thing." The first guy was Carl Furillo, a dangerous hitter and a tough cookie all around. One thing was sure,
Furillo wasn't going to give you anything. The familiar soft haze
that always hangs over the Stadium late in the day on World Series
afternoons was on Larsen's side, but Furillo had that bat in his hand
and he looked like a man who was planning to ambush somebody.
Carl fouled off two pitches, took a ball, fouled off two more into the
boxes back of first base, then hit a fast ball in the air to the right
fielder, Hank Bauer. One out. The next batter was Roy Campanella,
holder of the all-time National League record for the most home
runs by a catcher in a single season, big, brawny and as confident as
he was menacing. Roy swung at Larsen's first pitch and hit a long
foul into the upper left-field stands. It was foul by enough but it
shook up the crowd just the same. Larsen's second pitch to Campanella was a big-breaking curve ball and Roy obliged by hitting it
on the ground to Billy Martin at second base. Two out. Sal Maglie
was due up but everybody knew Walter Alston would go to a
pinch hitter, and he did. Dale Mitchell, the old Cleveland Indian
outfielder, came out of the Brooklyn dugout with a bat in his hand.
The Yankees knew Mitchell well from his Cleveland days. He was
a left-handed swinger and a slap hitter, a threat to splash a single
to any field at any time. "He really scared me up there," Larsen
said. "Looking back on it, though, I know how much strain *he* was
under. He must have been paralyzed. That made two of us."

Larsen wasn't so paralyzed, though, that he wasn't still able to
throw the ball in there as hard as he had been throwing it all day.
But the crowd groaned when Mitchell let the first pitch go by and
Pinelli called it a ball. Don, feeling the sweat running into his eyes
and down his back and soaking the palms of his hands, got the next
one over for a swinging strike. Next came another fast ball, outside,
then a foul into the stands for strike two. That made 96 pitches the
big fellow had thrown. He threw one more, a fast ball, waist high,

over the outside corner. Mitchell started to swing at it, then held back, and I don't think anybody in the whole big ball park took a breath until Babe Pinelli's hand shot up firmly to signal strike three.

That right arm of Pinelli's set off an explosion of emotion. Yogi catapulted out toward the mound as if he had been shot from a cannon. He didn't run up to Larsen, he jumped at him in the air. There wasn't anything Don could do except catch him and hold him and carry him all the way into the dugout like a 200-pound baby. Nobody had ever pitched a perfect game in a World Series before, so there was no book on how you were supposed to act when it happened. What everybody did, then, was to act pretty much like wild men. The Yankees' clubhouse was like Times Square on V-J day, the most somber man's emotions running riot in the general atmosphere of mass hysteria. You could almost forgive the out-of-town newspaperman who piped his voice high enough to carry over the heads of the tiers of reporters surrounding Casey Stengel and asked astonishingly, "Casey, do you think this was the best game Larsen ever pitched?" And certainly, if you remembered St. Petersburg and the automobile and the telephone pole, you could understand Del Webb saying cheerfully, "This will set spring training back ten years."

Just before the game Larsen had put the arm on traveling secretary Bill McCorry for a $200 advance against his World Series check. He was broke and he needed the money to buy an airplane ticket home to San Diego, where he expected to get a job for the winter months, maybe in the Sears, Roebuck store where he had worked before. Now, in the welter of excitement, he heard player agent Frank Scott tell him that he could make $100,000 in testimonials and appearances before the winter was over. (He really did make about $35,000, and he might have made more if he hadn't insisted on remaining Don Larsen and taking a little time out to have some fun.) Before he could shake loose, first from the clubhouse and then from his hotel room, for a night on the town, Don had agreed to a guest shot on the Bob Hope Show that would bring him in $7,500 right then and there, plus expenses which included a first-class airplane ticket to Los Angeles. He wouldn't need the $200 from Bill McCorry.

It was an astonishing change of fortune for a pitcher who just two seasons before had been the losingest pitcher in the American League. That was the first year the transplanted St. Louis Browns had played in Baltimore as the new Orioles, and Don did nothing to help convince the Baltimore fans that their new ball club was worth supporting. He was always as willing to pitch as he was to go out with the gang, but he won only 3 games and lost 21 that year. His manager, Jimmy Dykes, said bitterly, "The only thing Larsen fears is sleep." Don still had no reason to feel that there was any particular virtue in sleep. He went to bed early the night before his first Series start against the Dodgers and was belted out in the second inning. He stayed up late, drank his usual allotment of beer and had that post-midnight pizza pie, the night before The Perfect Game, and the moral didn't escape him. He has moved around quite a bit in baseball since the year of his glory, to the Kansas City Athletics, to the Chicago White Sox, to the minors, to the San Francisco Giants, but the last time he was heard from he was still staying up late and hoping for the best.

The man who held the center of the stage five years later is a different kind of personality. Roger Maris may not be "The Last Angry Man" that some of the baseball writers have labeled him but he is far from the happy-go-lucky, hail-fellow-well-met type. When people began to think, halfway through the 1961 season, that Maris had a chance to tie or break the most revered of all baseball records, Babe Ruth's 60 home runs in one season, a reporter approached him and asked if he really wanted to be the man to break the Ruth record. "Damn right," Rog said briefly. He didn't bother to wrap his answer in a lot of pious tributes to the Babe. He just told the truth. That's the way he has been all his life and he saw no reason to change just because there were a couple of dozen reporters asking him questions after every ball game, one set of questions if he hit another home run and another set if he didn't hit one. When the questions got too personal, or too stupid, Rog would freeze, and then the reporters would get mad and write things that would make him madder. Before the season was over Rog was having at least as much trouble with the newspapermen as he was with the pitchers of the American League, and maybe more.

It didn't help any, either, that some of the older men of the game seemed to see in Maris' assault on the Ruth record some sort of vague attack on Ruth himself. "It would be a shame," Rogers Hornsby said sarcastically, "if Ruth's record was broken by a .270 hitter." If that was supposed to put Rog in his place, it didn't. But it did in- flame his indignation about the treatment he was getting. "I don't understand why they all seem to think it would be an insult to Ruth's memory if I broke the record," he complained. "Nobody ever heard me say I was a better hitter than Babe Ruth. I'm not trying to be Babe Ruth, I'm just trying to hit sixty-one home runs and be Roger Maris. Why don't they leave me alone?"

There was, of course, no chance that they would leave him alone, and from the time he passed August 15 with 48 home runs to his credit and a month and a half left in which to get the last 13 he needed, there was bound to be more pressure on him instead of less. Not even the fact that Mickey Mantle, on August 16, had 45 home runs to Maris' 48, and had a very real chance to break the record himself, made things any easier for Roger. He was the pacesetter, and he remained the pacesetter all the way. For the first time in his career with the Yankees, Mickey was virtually left alone. He ad- mitted complacently that it made things a lot easier for him. "But it's rough on Rog," he said. "I wish they wouldn't get on him the way they do. It's tough. I know."

In the second game of a three-game series with the Tigers on the first weekend of September, Maris hit his 52nd and 53rd homers. It was Mantle's turn in the last game of the series. Mickey hit his

No. 49 and No. 50. By now, not only the city of New York but the whole country was excited by the young sluggers' race with the ghost of Babe Ruth. Mickey couldn't play in the Labor Day double-header with the Washington Senators because he had come up with a sore arm, and Rog was shut out without a hit in both games, but that just made the suspense more intense.

MARIS HITS 54, SEVEN GAMES AHEAD OF RUTH PACE. That's what the headlines said the day after Roger connected against the Senators on Wednesday, September 6. He made it 55 the next day against his old teammates, the Indians, and then, on Friday night, September 8, it was Mantle's turn, this time for No. 52. The Yankee fans shouted their heads off for both men every time they stepped up to bat. Even Maris, worn and irritated by the relentless pounding of his working-press inquisitors, responded emotionally to the uninhibited rooting. There were times when he just wished it was all over, wished that he could shake off the weight he had been carrying on his shoulders and just go off somewhere and sleep the sleep of the exhausted, but he kept trying and he kept swinging. He made it 56 on Saturday, September 9, with a booming shot off Jim Grant of the Indians. That was an especially meaningful home run for the M & M team because it gave Rog and Mickey 108 homers between them, one more than Babe Ruth and Lou Gehrig had hit in 1927, the year of Ruth's 60, more home runs than had been struck by any two men on one team in one season in the game's history.

But Rog still had four to go to tie Ruth and five to go to break the record. Mickey, after he added No. 53 in a Sunday double-header with the Indians, still needed seven to tie and eight to go ahead. Neither of them got anything in the September 12 game at Chicago, but Rog got numbers 57 and 58 in Detroit and headed for Baltimore trying desperately to ignore the big commotion in the papers over Commissioner Ford Frick's ruling that he would have to equal or break Ruth's record in 154 games, the classic schedule distance, if he was to be accorded equal billing with Ruth in the official record book. Any record he set in the last eight games of the new, 162-game schedule brought about by the league's expansion to ten clubs, would be recorded separately, Frick said—and the Ruth record would continue to stand. Many of the writers and a large percentage of the fans thought the ruling was unfair. "A season is a season," they argued. Rog said nothing. He just kept trying to hit home runs. When you have hit 58 home runs in 151 games, he figured, you ought to be able to hit two or three more in eleven games—and if he ended up the season with 61 home runs he would be glad to let the Commissioner and the writers quarrel about how to print the numbers in the record book.

It was all Maris now. Nobody even bothered to ask Mantle what he thought of his chances. Mickey kidded about it himself. "I already got my man," he said one day, referring to the fact that his 53 put him well ahead of Lou Gehrig's 47 the year of Ruth's 60. "It's up to Rog now to get the other guy." Rog didn't get anything in the twilight-night doubleheader the Yankees and Orioles played in Baltimore on September 19, and the next night, with Mantle put out of action by a sore throat, Roger played his 154th game of the season. It was an odd quirk of Fate that the milestone game should come in Baltimore, Babe Ruth's birthplace, but the fact that the fans seemed to be dead set against him didn't keep Maris from giving it the old pro's dead-game try. The first time up he hit a line drive to the right fielder, Earl Robinson. It was a good shot but there never was any question about its being caught. His next time at bat, in the third inning, Rog took a ball, swung and missed, took another ball, then drove his 59th home run into the right-field stands, about 400 feet from home plate.

Back home in Raytown, Missouri, a suburb of Kansas City, Roger's wife watched him hit No. 59 on television. KMBC-TV, the American Broadcasting Company outlet in Kansas City, had set up a special closed-circuit showing in its studio just for her benefit. With six innings still to go, Rog figured to get up at least twice

more, and everybody knew he might very well do it. Actually, he
had three more chances, but he struck out, hit a fly ball to center
field, and grounded out to the pitcher. He was disappointed, but he
kept it to himself. The Yankees had clinched the pennant, he had
hit his 59th home run, and things, he figured, could be a lot worse.
Roger was as happy as anybody at the midnight victory party the
Yankee owners staged in the Lord Baltimore Hotel, with cham-
pagne and T-bone steak for all, a hillbilly singing act by pitcher
Jim Coates for entertainment, the first pennant-winning rookie
manager in Yankee history as the guest of honor, and Maris' 59th
home run as the icing on the cake.

You could, that night, sit down with a piece of paper, a pencil
and a *Little Red Book of Baseball,* and list the champion home-run
hitters of baseball for all time, the men who had hit 50 or more
homers in a single season. You would start off with Babe Ruth, who
hit 60 in 1927 and 59 in 1921. Then, second on your list, you would
write down the name of Roger Maris, who had hit 59 already in
1961. There wouldn't be many other names on your list—Jimmie
Foxx, for his 58 in 1932 and his 50 in 1938; Hank Greenberg, for
his 58 in 1938; Hack Wilson, for his 56 in 1930; Ralph Kiner, for
his 54 in 1949 and his 51 in 1947; Mickey Mantle, for his 53 in
1961 and his 52 in 1956; Johnny Mize, for his 51 in 1947; and
Willie Mays, for his 51 in 1955. It was pretty good company Roger
was keeping. But he still hungered for those two more home runs.
He had the fever, and he didn't mind admitting it.

He didn't have the Babe Ruth fever so much, though, that he
was willing to throw his money away simply to flatter his own ego.
The 59th home-run ball he hit in Baltimore was caught by an un-
employed machine operator, Bob Reitz, who was escorted into the
Yankees' dressing room in Baltimore to meet Maris by a crowd of
reporters and photographers. Reitz told Maris that he could have
the ball for two sets of tickets to the World Series, worth about $60,
and an all-expense trip to New York for the Series games, which

would cost Roger at least another $500. "Nothing doing," Rog said bluntly. "I'd like to have the ball, but it isn't worth that kind of money to me."

Mickey Mantle stole a quick headline from Roger on Saturday, September 23, when he hit his 54th homer at Boston. But Maris wasn't through yet. He made it 60 against the Orioles at Yankee Stadium on Sunday, and that one was an authentic wallop into the upper right-field stands. Then, in the last game of the year, the 162nd game on the schedule, against the Red Sox at the Stadium, Rog leaned into one of rookie Tracy Stallard's fast balls and, in Stallard's own words, "knocked the stuffing out of it." Roger didn't have to worry about being held up by the retriever of his historic 61st home run because a Sacramento, California, restaurant owner named Sam Gordon already had offered a $5,000 reward for it, and the young man who caught it, Sal Durante, a nineteen-year-old Brooklyn truck driver, was only too glad to go along with Gordon's publicity stunt. But, more important, the chase was over, the hunt was at an end. Beating the Cincinnati Reds in the World Series seemed easy, and then Roger could clean out his locker and say good-by to the reporters and the advertising agency hustlers and the ten percent men and go back home for the winter. It was all over. It might never happen again, for Roger or anybody else, but it was over for now. "I'm happy," Roger said, on friendly terms with the newspapermen for the first time in weeks. "It's a good feeling." Even Tracy Stallard, experiencing the rare feeling of occupying the center of the stage in the Red Sox dressing room, was philosophical about it. "I'll tell you this much," he said, "he hit sixty home runs off some pretty good pitchers before he got to me. I'm not ashamed. Anyway, maybe this will push up my price on the banquet circuit."

It certainly pushed up Maris' price, just as Frank Scott had predicted. Whether or not Roger made as much money that winter as Frank had predicted he might, no one else will ever know. Scottie had guessed $100,000 for Don Larsen and Larsen had ended up with $35,000. In what probably was a rash moment and might have been an inaccurate quote, he had said something about 61 home runs being worth half a million dollars to Maris. The chances are Rog is still a long way shy of that figure, but it's equally sure he has no thought of complaining. The name of Roger Maris, like the name of Don Larsen, will endure long after both men have left the game, long after the figures in their bank accounts have ceased to matter. You may not be able to buy houses, automobiles or yachts with a Perfect Game or 61 home runs, but you can't spend them, either. They last forever.

Chapter 11

There isn't any more money left
in the game. Musial and Berra
already got it all.—JOE GARAGIOLA

TEN or eleven years ago in Florida, during spring
training, some of the old-time baseball writers began playing a
game during long car or bus trips from one spring-camp town to
another. They called it "L. Peter B." It was a simple enough game,
if you followed baseball closely and were a sufficiently dedicated
reader of the guides and record books to know the full names of
all the big-league ballplayers. The idea was that your opponent
gave you the first initial, middle name and last initial of a ballplayer, and you had to identify him. The name of the game was
"L. Peter B." because that, standing for Lawrence Peter Berra of
the Yankees, was considered to be just about the easiest name of all
to guess. Not much harder would be S. Frank M., for Stanley Frank
Musial, and not the least of the reasons why these names are the
easiest is because their owners stayed around the big leagues as active
players for such a long time. As E. Bradsher S. (for Enos Slaughter)
so eloquently expressed it when he said, "I'll never quit; they'll have

to tear my uniform off," these two baseball greats were not only durable, they loved to play and they hated to quit.

Stan Musial wasn't the only one who had a hard time containing his emotions the day in midsummer of 1963 when he told the members of the St. Louis Cardinal family, at their annual outing on owner Gussie Busch's farm, that he wouldn't be coming back to play in 1964. Stan's way of saying good-by was typically Musial: "Baseball has been my life. I've loved St. Louis and this ball club, and I've had fun all these years." You knew he was telling the truth. Nobody ever enjoyed playing ball more than Stan did. Despite his awesome stature as one of the game's immortals, a giant among hitters and team players whose election to the Hall of Fame is a mere formality awaiting the first year in which he will be eligible under the rule requiring a five-year absence from the game as an active player, there is an appealing boyishness about Musial. He is one of the handful of superstars ever to be paid $100,000 for a single season of baseball but he admits that he would have played for room and board if that had been the only way he could have done it, and he giggles as though he thinks it's a big joke that he has made so much money out of the game. Stan does not have it in him to take himself seriously.

I remember reading some years ago an article by the novelist Jerome Weidman, who told about playing ball with his two sons and a few other young boys on a St. Petersburg beach one windy March day when a tall stranger in a blue sweater saved their ball from rolling into the ocean and then stayed around to show the kids the right way to swing a bat. The kids were completely taken by him, and Weidman was grateful, but inwardly a little hurt, too, that he had lost the attention of the boys. Then, abruptly, the big stranger handed the bat to Weidman. "Sorry," he said shyly, "I didn't mean to hog the show." And this, Weidman found out the next day when the kids discovered their benefactor's identity and got his autograph, was Stan Musial, who ended his career the pos-

sessor of seven National League batting championships, three Most
Valuable Player awards, and at least seven different batting, fielding and endurance records. No wonder they called him, with simple
respect, The Man.

It was the fans in Brooklyn, where Musial used to hit .500 or so
in every series against the Dodgers, who hung that nickname on
him, but it was adopted by virtually everybody almost overnight
because it was so obviously right for him. "Banjo" is what his old
friend Bob Broeg, the St. Louis sports editor and Musial's biog-
rapher, calls him—short for banjo hitter, baseball jargon for the
man who hits singles rather than the long ball. Stan himself likes
to say he was "just a little ol' singles hitter," but both he and Broeg
are kidding. It is true that Musial was noted more for his consistently high batting averages than for his home-run totals, but
he hit 30 or more home runs six times and finished his career with
475 homers, not far from Mel Ott's National League record of 511.

One of the standard jokes in every baseball after-dinner speaker's repertoire is the one Joe Garagiola made famous. "What's the
best way to pitch to Musial? That's easy. Walk him and then try
to pick him off first base."

No matter how you look at Stan Musial's story you have to conclude that if he hadn't existed in real life Horatio Alger or somebody would have had to invent him. The son of an immigrant
Polish coal miner, Stan grew up in Donora, Pennsylvania, a mining
town famous for its thick and sometimes poisonous smog. His father
wanted him to go to college on an athletic scholarship, not go into
professional baseball, but when Stan's mother joined the argument
on the boy's side, Stan won and got his chance. He was a pitcher in
those days, and all the arguing almost went for nothing when he
hurt his shoulder doing an off-day stint in the outfield. He tried to
make a shoestring catch and fell heavily on his shoulder. He didn't
know it for some months but his pitching career was ended. It was
a good thing Stan already had showed that he could hit; otherwise

he might have been sent back home to work in the mines or in his new father-in-law's grocery store. Instead, he got a chance to make it as an outfielder, and in the summer of 1941 Musial moved from Springfield to Rochester to St. Louis, from Class C to the major leagues all in one season. He hit .426 for the Cardinals in 12 games at the tail end of the season and was a big-leaguer from then on.

It must have been five or six years later, when Stan had come back from the navy and was doing business at the same old stand, putting the fear of God into the pitchers of the National League, that umpire Larry Goetz watched him slide into home plate at the end of an inside-the-park home run and shook his head admiringly after signaling him safe. "Stanley," Goetz said, "I've been meaning to tell you this for some time. I think you're a professional hitter." Musial reacts badly to most compliments. He blushes and giggles and changes the subject as quickly as he can. But he didn't this time. He grinned his boyish grin and agreed with Goetz. "I think I'll make the grade," he said.

He made it, all right. Once he hit five home runs in a double-header against the Giants at the Polo Grounds. In two back-to-back games at Ebbets Field he destroyed the Dodgers with nine hits, including a home run, a triple, three doubles and four singles, in 11 times at bat. In the season of 1958 he became the eighth man in all the long history of baseball to accumulate more than 3,000 base hits. Once, against the Cincinnati Reds, he struck out but got all the way to second base before the catcher, who had let the ball go through his legs, could retrieve it. "That's Musial for you," manager Bucky Walters of the Reds complained. "You strike him out and he still gets two bases."

"Ooh," the fans moaned in every ball park around the league when Musial stepped into the batter's box, the big number 6 showing bold and clear on the back of his uniform, "here comes The Man again." And Stan would take up his distinctive stance, feet close together, bat held straight up over his shoulder, back arched, body coiled, looking for all the world, Ted Lyons once said, "like a kid peeking around the corner to see if the cop was coming."

Bob Broeg says one of his favorite Musial stories happened after one of the rare games at Ebbets Field in which Stan didn't hit. He was in what for him passed as a slump. But at least this day he had helped the ball club with three sensational catches in the outfield, the last one a particularly spectacular tumbling catch that saved the game for the Cardinals. "Stash," Terry Moore told Musial in the locker room after the game, "what a ballplayer you would be if you could only hit."

The *Sporting News* knew what it was doing when it selected Musial as the winner, in 1956, of its first Player of the Decade award, covering the years from 1946 to 1956. "I can't hit like Ted Williams," Stan said in his acceptance speech, "I can't field like Joe DiMaggio, and I can't pitch like Bob Feller, but I thank you deeply for this high honor." He also remembered that way back in his rookie season somebody had written a newspaper story saying that this kid Musial was off to an impressive start as a hitter but that, "with that crazy stance, he'll never last." He lasted twenty-two years, a long time in a young man's game, and he was still a danger-ous hitter and a good one in his last season. "Musial hitting," the Cardinals' old coach, Buzzy Wares, said, "is like a finicky house-wife shopping. Did you ever see a woman looking for the best tomatoes in a bin? She'll feel one, pinch another, squeeze a third. That's Musial at the plate, sorting through the pitches, looking for the one that's just right. And when he finds the ripe one, look out!"

Stan found a couple of ripe ones the day his son Dick made him a grandfather for the first time. That was on Wednesday, September 11, 1963. Stan found out before the game that Dick's wife had given birth to a baby boy, and he broke out the box of cigars he had been keeping in his locker at Busch Stadium in anticipation of the occasion. Then he really celebrated by hitting a two-run homer, the 474th home run of his major-league career, and a run-scoring single to help the Cardinals beat the Cubs, 8–0, and stay just three games behind the league-leading Dodgers in a close pennant race. When the Dodgers, down to a one-game lead, met the Cardinals head to head at Busch Stadium in an all-or-nothing series, the only St. Louis run scored in the first game was on a home run by 42-year-old Stanley Frank Musial, brand-new grandfather.

The whole country rejoiced with Stan when he took dead aim on the 3,000-hit club with a big day in a doubleheader with the Reds in St. Louis on May 11, 1958. The five hits he picked up that day put his lifetime total at 2,998, just two short of the magic number. When he got one hit in the first game of a two-game series in Chicago, Stan remarked to his manager, Freddie Hutchinson, that he almost hoped he would draw a walk every time up the next day because after that game they would be going back home and nothing would make him happier than to get his 3,000th hit in St. Louis. Hutch thought about it overnight and made up his mind not to play Stan the next day unless he really needed him. It was a decision that provoked a lot of criticism in the newspapers, but Hutch stuck to his guns. He did, that is, until the sixth inning, when he had a chance to get back into the ball game. The Cubs were leading, 3–1, Gene Green was on second with a double, and there was one out when Hutchinson called Musial in from the bullpen where he was sunning himself and swapping stories with the relief pitchers. Stan ran in to the dugout, took one of his thin-handled, 34-ounce bats out of the rack, and went up to hit against right-hander Moe Drabowsky. The count went to two balls and two strikes before Stan leaned into a curve ball that hung a little and drilled it into left field for a double.

The crowd cheered almost as loudly as a St. Louis crowd might have done. Umpire Frank Dascoli retrieved the ball and walked over and handed it to Musial. Hutch came out of the dugout to shake Stan's hand and take him out of the game for a pinch runner. Musial stopped at the field box occupied by his wife, Lil, and some friends from home, kissed Lil happily, and retired to the clubhouse to think about his name being bracketed now forever with the names of Ty Cobb, Tris Speaker, Honus Wagner, Napoleon Lajoie, Eddie Collins, Cap Anson and Paul Waner. Actually, Stan had already celebrated the big event a couple of days early. He and his restaurant partner, Biggie Garagnani, had scheduled a 3,000-hit party for the night of the doubleheader with the Reds, and when Stan failed to make the figure that day, they decided to go ahead and have the party anyway. "It's the first time," Jim Toomey of the Cardinals said, "I ever heard of a three-thousand-hit party marked down to two thousand, nine hundred and ninety-eight." But it didn't take Musial long to make up the difference.

Stan always pays his debts. Nobody knew that better than Dickie Kerr. The old Chicago White Sox pitcher, winner of two games for the Black Sox in the 1919 World Series despite the fact that eight of his teammates had contracted to throw the Series, was his manager at Daytona Beach in 1940 and had more to do with keeping Stan in baseball than anyone except his wife. Stan's shoulder injury had ruined him as a pitcher, and his first reaction was that he would have to quit, go back home and get a job. Lil was going to have a baby and it was no time to be fooling around trying to play a game he could no longer play. But Kerr, convinced that Stan could make it as an outfielder, not only talked him into staying with the club but even took him and Lil into his own house so that their expenses would be smaller and Mrs. Kerr would be there to help Lil when the baby came. Years later, when Stan was at his peak, he bought a house in Florida for the Kerrs and told them it was theirs for as long as they lived. Nobody ever would have known he had done it if Dickie Kerr, in his understandable pride in his old friend and protégé, hadn't mentioned it to a Florida newspaperman, who couldn't resist passing the story on to the world.

Dickie Musial—named after Kerr—said it best when he was only eight years old and was talking to a visitor to the house. "How do you like having a father who's a ballplayer?" the visitor wanted to know. "Swell," Dickie said honestly. "He must be pretty good, too, because at school, when they choose up sides, the kids always say, 'I'll take Musial.' Do you know my daddy very well?" The visitor said, no, he didn't, and asked, "Will you tell me what he's like?" Dickie nodded enthusiastically. "I like him," he said very seriously. "He's a real nice guy."

S. Frank M. looks every inch the part of a baseball immortal. Lean, rangy, ruggedly handsome, he could pose for a classic painting of The Athlete. L. Peter B. is a different sort entirely. This is a man about whom the bench jockeys used to make cracks like, "How does your wife like living in a tree?" But the indisputable fact that Yogi Berra is physically homely, not only in his gnomish features but even in his magnificently coordinated athlete's body, never interfered with his ability to punish a baseball with a bat or to play the game in the field with the easy skill of the natural ballplayer. It didn't prevent him from enjoying a remarkably long life as a major-leaguer. "Nobody ever hit a baseball with his face," Yogi always said patiently. And it didn't deter the businesslike Yankee owners from delighting their millions of fans by appointing him manager of the ball club at the end of the 1963 season. Even the professional Yankee-haters scattered throughout the country applauded Yogi's promotion. He is everybody's favorite.

The first time Yogi ever stepped up to bat in an American League ball game was in 1946. He had played 77 games that year for Newark and his .314 batting average had earned him an end-of-season trial with the Yankees. His first time up he hit a home run, and he ended his brief big-league season with a .364 average. Seventeen years later, two stories in the New York newspapers a week apart in the month of July, 1963, testified to Yogi Berra's durability. He wasn't the Yankees' first string catcher any more, having given way to Elston Howard, who was on his way to becoming the Most Valuable Player in the American League. Yogi had, in fact, already played through a couple of seasons as a spare outfielder and pinch hitter. But now, although Roy Hamey, the about-to-retire general manager, had said three years before that he didn't think Yogi would ever again catch a regular league game for the Yankees, he was doing exactly that in his extremely well-paid role of part-time coach and number two catcher. On Sunday, June 30, the Yankees took both games of a doubleheader at the Stadium from the Red Sox, and Yogi was the anchor man in the key inning of each game. He hit a three-run home run in the first inning of the opener, provoking manager Johnny Pesky of the Red Sox to complain, "Berra hasn't played a game in two weeks, so he comes in and hits a home run in the first inning. What are you going to do with a guy like that?" Then, in the second game, Yogi drew a second-inning pinch-hitting walk. When Tony Kubek whacked a grounder past Dick Stuart at first base, and the ball bounced wildly off the fence and trickled out to the outfield, the two base runners ahead of Yogi scored easily and the great man himself chugged around third with a full head of steam and slid home safely in a belly-whopper slide reminiscent of Pepper Martin at his best. At the advanced baseball age of thirty-eight, Yogi had come through with the big play in both games of the doubleheader. A week later he wrecked one of Early Wynn's bids for his 300th victory by hitting a game-winning three-run home run to help the Yankees beat the Indians, 11–6. Maybe he was all washed up as a regular, but washed-up ballplayers who can hit like that and run the bases like that are hard to find.

Yogi has always been one in a million. He grew up in a tiny house on Elizabeth Avenue in the old Italian section of St. Louis known as The Hill. Yogi lived with his mother, father, sister and three brothers in a scrupulously kept house at number 5447, right across the street from number 5446, where the Garagiola family, including young Joey, lived. Joey was Yogi's best friend. "I don't know what the odds were that the two of us kids, living across the street from each other on the same little block, would grow up to become big-league catchers," Yogi said years later, "but considering the fact that there were only sixteen first-string catchers in both leagues when we broke in, they must have been pretty big odds."

They were, and they still are, even though there are ten ball clubs in each league now instead of only eight. The two boys played on the same neighborhood teams for years, mostly for the Stags A.C., which was supported by its members through judicious investments in the corner store's pinball machine and the sale of single Twenty Grand cigarettes, which cost ten cents a pack, for a penny apiece, thus achieving a 100 percent profit. Then, in 1946, Joey Garagiola caught for the St. Louis Cardinals and batted .314 in the World Series against the Red Sox. And in 1947 Yogi Berra caught and played the outfield for the New York Yankees in the World Series against the Dodgers, and even hit the first pinch-hit home run in Series history. The two kids from Elizabeth Avenue had come a long way. Long enough so that Bill McGowan, the umpire, sent a couple of baseballs into the Yankee clubhouse with a request for Yogi to autograph them. When they came back to him neatly signed "Larry Berra," McGowan stared at them and walked straight into the clubhouse and confronted Berra with them. "Who the hell put this Larry Berra on these balls?" he demanded. "What's the matter, you couldn't sign the balls yourself?"

"That's my name," Yogi said, puzzled.

"The hell it is," McGowan said. "Sign them Yogi. Ain't that your name, Yogi?"

Yogi shrugged his shoulders. "Well," he said, "if it wasn't before, I guess it is now."

It is and it has been ever since one of his boyhood friends, Jack Maguire, who had a short hitch as an infielder with the Giants, pinned the nickname on him after the gang had gone to the movies and had seen a short subject that was a travelogue about India and that had some scenes of a Hindu fakir who was called a yogi. Maguire told Berra, when they went outside after the picture, "You know, you look just like that yogi. That's what I'm going to call you, Yogi." And it stuck.

There are all kinds of Yogi Berra stories, and some of them are

even true. Jimmy Cannon tells a couple that go back to Yogi's first
full season with the Yankees, 1947. "I got to know Yogi a little in
spring training down in St. Pete," Jimmy says, "and the first night
back in New York I was interested when I saw him sitting alone
after dinner in the lobby of the Hotel Edison just off Broadway.
'Hey, Yog,' I said to him, 'aren't you going out anywhere tonight?
After all, this is your first night in New York as a full-fledged
Yankee. You ought to do something to celebrate.' 'Aah,' Yogi said,
hardly looking up from his paper, 'what's there to do in this town,
anyway?' "

Jimmy also likes to tell about the trouble Yogi had getting from
midtown Manhattan to Ebbets Field for exhibition games that first
spring with the Yankees. The ball club gave all the new players
printed instructions carefully detailing how best to make the trip,
but the day of the first game with the Dodgers, Yogi was late, and
everybody gave him a hard time about it. Cannon was in the
Yankees' dressing room an hour or so before the second game, and
when he saw Yogi sitting in front of his locker, he said, "Con-
gratulations, Yogi. I see you made it. You finally figured out the
subways, huh?" "No," Yogi said honestly, "I knew I was gonna
take the wrong train, so I left an hour early."

From his first years with the Yankees it was clear that Berra
was going to be one of the good ones, so it shouldn't have surprised
anyone that he quickly became interested in being paid for what
he could do. More than one sportswriter and broadcaster noticed
that Yogi, a bad-ball hitter who hates to pass up the first pitch
thrown to him no matter where it is, had no trouble at all passing
up the first contract mailed to him by the Yankee front office. He
waged his first serious holdout in the spring of 1950, and it was a
lulu. Shortly after the contracts were put into the mail that February, a reporter hungry for a scoop asked Yogi if he had signed his
yet. "Nope," Yogi said cheerfully. "What did you do? Send it back?"
"Yeah, I sent it back," Yogi said. "Wasn't it for enough money?"

"No, it wasn't." "How much was it for? Are you far apart?" "I don't know." "What do you mean, you don't know? Didn't you look at it?" "No, I didn't. I just told my wife to mail the first one right back to them. I knew it wouldn't be for enough." And that's when the Yankees first discovered what they were up against in Yogi Berra.

At the same time, of course, they were discovering what they had in Yogi. In 1950 Yogi caught 151 games for the Yankees, batted .322 and accounted for 124 runs batted in. His 192 hits included 28 home runs, 6 triples and 30 doubles. He was the American League's all-star catcher and any club in either league would gladly have paid a small fortune for him. The $18,000 he had earned in 1950 didn't strike him as enough by a long shot, so he settled upon $40,000 as a fair figure for his new contract. "We're offering him $25,000," George Weiss said, "and when he comes down out of the clouds we'll be happy to bargain with him." As matters turned out, they were happy to bargain with him exactly twenty-four hours later, for $30,000, which meant that Yogi had got himself a $12,000 raise. "Didn't Weiss get mad?" one interviewer asked Yogi. "Sure, he did," Yogi said, "but I got pretty mad myself."

The legend of Yogi Berra is unique in big-league baseball because it involves a man who is credited with immense ability and, at the same time, immense naïveté. The truth, of course, is that Yogi is every bit as able and nowhere near as naïve as they say he is. Yogi has done a good job of capitalizing on the assets God gave him. He ended his playing career with a lifetime batting average of .285; he hit 358 home runs, more than any other catcher in history; and he made more money than any other catcher. He had the good fortune to play for the Yankees, in New York, over a long span of years, and he was able to store away a great deal of money from sideline activities including a $400,000 bowling alley he built with Phil Rizzuto in 1960. He lives in a thirty-year-old mansion in Montclair, New Jersey, which looks like the baronial home of a Wall Street banker. He has a swimming pool in the back yard and he plays golf at one of New Jersey's finest golf clubs. He owns a small piece of the Yoo Hoo Chocolate Drink Company, which may not be exactly a rival of Coca-Cola but is a going business which will pay handsome dividends to him for many years to come. Few ballplayers of the day have earned more money than Yogi Berra.

Part of it he earned by what he did to one pitcher in two World Series. Yogi wrecked the Dodgers' Don Newcombe in 1955 and 1956 and just about left him for dead. He clubbed ten hits and batted .417 in 1955, then came back with three home runs and ten runs batted in in 1956. Both times his chief victim was big Newk, a fastballing right-hander good enough to be a 27-game winner in the National League in '56.

Some of Yogi's success stems from his personality. He makes friends with everybody, he says funny things and he says wise things in a funny way, he looks like everybody's homely cousin, and practically every baseball fan of his time likes him. They liked him even when he was killing their favorite team with his wicked drives over the right-field wall. The fans remember things like Yogi's being interviewed on radio after his marriage to beautiful Carmen Short, a non-Italian, non-Hill girl from the Missouri farm country. "Isn't your mother going to be unhappy that you didn't marry a girl from The Hill?" the broadcaster wondered. "Nope," Yogi said, "she likes Carm. Anyway, those girls on The Hill, they had their chance." They also remember things like his needling Hank Aaron of the Braves when Aaron came to bat in a World Series and Yogi noticed that he was holding his bat with the label facing the wrong way. "Hey, Hank," Yogi said, "you're going to bust that bat. You got the label out instead of in." "Never mind," Aaron said, "I ain't up here to read, I'm up here to hit."

Yogi has come so far that even Frank Crosetti, the Yankees' silent man, who is staying on as one of manager Yogi's coaches, makes jokes about him. In the television coup of the century, Jerry Coleman persuaded the extraordinarily reticent Crosetti to share a post-game show with Yogi after one of the Yankees' home games in the late summer of 1963. During the conversation Jerry suggested to Yogi that he must have a sackful of records to his credit by now. "Yeah," Crosetti said dryly, "and he has a sackful of money, too."

He spends it, too. Herbert Warren Wind, the golf expert, has a story about that. "Yogi," says Wind, "had played a round at his club with two friends from New York who wanted to go after-ward from the club to Yogi and Phil's bowling alley. It was ar-ranged that Yogi would lead the way in his car and his friends would follow in theirs. 'There are two tolls,' Yogi warned them. 'You'll need a quarter for the first one and a dime for the second one. Okay?' Everybody nodded in understanding, and the caravan set off. A few minutes later Yogi swung his car into an entrance to the Garden State Parkway. He paid the toll and talked a little while to the tollgate attendant. As he pulled away his friends drove up behind him and the driver held out his hand with the required quarter. But the attendant waved him on. 'Mr. Berra,' he said, 'has already taken care of it.' "

Yogi is a relentless competitor. Once he heard a siren behind him as he headed home from Yankee Stadium, and he decided to make a run for it. The law didn't catch up to him for miles, and when he was collared, the cop, embarrassed, said, "Gee, Yogi, I knew it was you all the time. All I wanted was your autograph for my kid."

A lot of people have wanted Yogi's autograph for a good many years. He holds more World Series records than any other ball-player. Toward the end of his career he set a record every time he played in a Series game, every time he went to bat in a Series game, every time he made a hit in a Series game. He did so well in so many World Series that people tend to forget that in his first one, in 1947, he was something of a flop. "Never," Connie Mack said, "have I seen worse ketchin' in a World Series." Yogi started the

Series as a catcher, was a pinch hitter in the middle, and finished it as an outfielder. He covered himself with glory by becoming the first man ever to pinch-hit a home run in the Series, but his batting average was only .158, with three hits in six games, and he was charged with two official and a few unofficial errors. It is as much a measure of Yogi's determination as of his ability that he was able to overcome that painful beginning to become one of the great hitters and fielders of Series history.

It is also part of Yogi's story that he has been able to rise above all the Berra jokes. "People seem to find it hard to believe," he said once, "but basically I'm a very serious person. It wasn't just luck that I became a ballplayer. I never wanted to be anything else and I never considered being anything else. I worked my tail off for it. To say that I don't have any worries or nerves is the opposite of the truth. I worry about getting old, I worry about not being able to get around on the fast ball any more, I worry about getting hurt, about keeping Carm happy, about the kids growing up good, and about staying out of trouble with God. I worry a lot."

His wife, Carmen, helps keep him on an even keel. Yogi likes to tell about the day he came home from the ball park grumbling because he had had a bad day. "We got beat," he told his wife, "and not only did we get beat but the umps were on me all day and I went for the collar." Carmen was unimpressed. "You're the one who's playing ball," she said, "not me. Don't tell me your troubles. You want me to tell you all about the kids and the house?"

Maybe the best insight into Yogi's success in baseball is what he has said about it himself. "I don't think there's anything better that a man could say about his life than that there's nothing else he would rather be than what he is. If you can say that and mean it, you've got it made. Don't get me wrong. I'm not bragging that being Yogi Berra is so great, what I mean is that I've been blessed with being the only thing I ever wanted to be since I was a kid, a big-league ballplayer, and I wouldn't trade places with anybody.

I'd rather be the Yankees' catcher than the President, and that makes me pretty lucky because I could never be the President but I've been the Yankees' catcher, or anyway I've been in their lineup, for more than two thousand ball games."

When he told the assembled press corps on the day of his coronation as manager that he was firing himself as a player and would do all of his managing from the bench, Yogi could look back on a total of exactly 2,116 games as a Yankee, more than have been played by any other Yankee except Lou Gehrig, whose string stretched to 2,164. He could look ahead to the inevitable mixture of pleasures and headaches that go with the job of managing any major-league ball club, even one so consistently victorious as the Yankees. He could think about how hard it was going to be to follow in the footsteps of the matchless Stengel and the efficient Houk, who won three pennants and two world championships in his three seasons as manager and would have had a perfect record if the club he himself labeled the best Yankee team he had ever had hadn't inexplicably blown the 1963 World Series to the charged-up Dodgers in four straight games. He could take pride in the flood of good wishes that all but engulfed him after his appointment was announced. And he could rest assured that, whether or not he ended up winning as many pennants as Houk had, he could be certain of one thing—he would at least sound more like Stengel than the more self-contained Major ever did. Nobody beats Yogi when it comes to making newspaper copy. He doesn't have to stop to think up any of his Stengel-type lines; they just come to him naturally.

"You can observe a lot by just watchin'," he said, talking about the experience he had picked up as a player-coach.

What makes a good manager? "A good ball club," Yogi said quickly.

Of a certain restaurant he used to frequent but doesn't now, Yogi said, "Nobody goes there any more because it's so overcrowded all the time."

Would he manage like Stengel or would he manage like Houk? "I'll manage like Yogi Berra," he said seriously. Then he made his way out of the big room the Yankees had hired for his press conference in the ritzy Savoy Hilton Hotel on Fifth Avenue, rode a cab to another hotel in which the Topps bubble-gum people were giving a dinner to baseball's rookies of the year, stepped up to the microphone when toastmaster Joe Garagiola called for him, looked around and said, "What's new?"

There is always something new in baseball. The Yankees have a new manager named Yogi Berra, the new pitching genius of the game is a good-looking young Dodger named Sandy Koufax, the Mets have a new ball park. The game is never the same and it is always the same. When Yogi and Stan Musial were young, the old-timers were Bob Feller and Joe DiMaggio. When Feller and DiMaggio were young, the old-timers were Frank Frisch and Lou Gehrig. When Frisch and Gehrig were young, the old-timers were Ty Cobb and Tris Speaker. The names change, the faces change, the ball parks change and the cities change. Some people say even the ball changes. But the game doesn't. There is an enduring magic about it, the geometric patterns of the infield, the contrasting white and gray of the home and the road uniforms, the graceful windup of the pitcher and the menacing tension of the batter poised to swing; the heavy-haunched, squatting catcher, the alert, quick-handed infielders and the surefooted outfielders with their powerful throwing arms, all ready to defend against the batted ball no matter where it might go. There is a surge of participation for everyone as the manager motions his infield in to guard against the base runner on third coming home on a ground ball. Everyone in the stands, layman or professional, is at such a moment a manager himself, agreeing or disagreeing with the strategy, considering and rejecting alternatives. Then the pitcher throws and the batter swings and the ball is smashed out to the left of the shortstop and everybody knows that if he had been playing back in his normal position he would have had the ball in his hip pocket. But now, with less than four seconds in which to make the play, he must scramble desperately to his left, dive for and clutch the darting baseball, straighten up and make his throw in time to beat out the determined runner, who, head down and knees pumping and heart pounding with strain, can cover the 30 yards down the line in just about 3.7 or 3.8 seconds. The ball slaps into the outstretched mitt of the first-baseman and the cleated foot of the runner bites into the canvas of the base. The entire tableau is suspended for a breathless moment as the game hangs in the balance. Then the crouching umpire gives the signal, the runner is either safe or he is out, and the game goes on—the game of the fan who is yelling himself hoarse for the hero who is doing it not only for the team, not only for the money, but for him, for the fan.

Because when Willie Mays runs out from under his cap to make a highway-robbery catch in center field, when Mickey Mantle, limping and battered from one injury after another, comes out of the dugout to pinch-hit with two men on and the Yankees three runs behind and smashes the ball high and far over the outfield fence to tie it up, when Sandy Koufax strikes out the last man in the last half of the last inning to win another one for the Dodgers, it is the fan, the popeyed, leather-lunged, ever-loving fan, who is making the catch, hitting the home run, throwing the strikeout pitch.

That's what baseball is all about.

ABOUT THE AUTHOR

Perhaps the country's best-known sports announcer, Mel Allen and his famous phrase, "How about that," are familiar to all football and baseball fans. With time out only for the war, he has been the Voice of the Yankees for twenty-five years, ever since 1939, and has broadcast innumerable All-Star baseball games, World Series, and football games.

Mel Allen was born in Birmingham, Alabama, the son of Julius and Anna Israel. He received his A.B. degree from the University of Alabama in 1932 and his LL.B. from the same school in 1936. As an instructor at Alabama, he taught speech and was debating coach from 1932 to 1937. In 1937 he became staff announcer for CBS.

During the war Mr. Allen served with the infantry and immediately after with the Armed Forces Radio Service for a year. He was discharged with the rank of staff sergeant.

Extremely active in philanthropic and charity work, he was chairman of the sports division of the Boy Scouts of America, worked for the Cerebral Palsy Fund, the Greater New York Fund, and the Fight for Sight campaign.

During 1950–51 Mr. Allen was president of the Sports Broadcasters Association. He is a member of the American Legion and Jewish War Veterans of the U.S.A.

Along with Frank Graham, Jr., Mr. Allen wrote *It Takes Heart*. His latest book, written with Ed Fitzgerald, is *You Can't Beat the Hours*.

Format by Katharine Sitterly

Set in Linotype Garamond

Composed, printed and bound by American Book–Stratford Press

HARPER & ROW, PUBLISHERS, INCORPORATED